III

Poetry and Truth

*

an essay

*

Traumear

Paperback ISBN 978-0-244-43307-9

*

www.traumear.com

*

Rather than writing about poetry and poems, I make amends and pit myself against some time-honoured prejudices, especially in myself, as I show what can be achieved both poetically and philosophically, as I remain mindful of our human need for coming to terms with our existential impoverishment in view of available spiritual riches.

This essay is conceived as number three in a set of four, after Poetry and beauty and Poetry and Poems and before Poetry and Technique.

*

(The end of poetry is

the eternity of the inner man.)

Poetry and Truth

If the intensities of feeling in me
could be discovered to have a name
rather than appearing and disappearing,
crudely now, under some guise of
illicit love-making, steeped in
overwhelming excuses for a settlement,
suddenly upon us, my friend,
or enough to make a saint wretched,
so tragically streaming with tears
or manacled to a modernist life –
I would stretch out my hand more wisely,
would ascertain the fitness of things
with a greater investment of love
and no callous brain would disrupt me,
no interrogation of bird song along
lines of moral correctness would chide me,
considering the role you would play
in the dark, trembling, hidden reaches
of my surprised, awful sensibility,
because here the magnitude of truth – reigns.

*

Anyone with a responsible interest in poetry, with a love and affection for it and an inclination to cherish the products of the poetic
sensibility, can probably recall his first contacts with the experience,
and in my own case what I remember most vividly, and with grati-

1

tude, is how poetry seemed to afford me the opportunity for truthfulness. I can honestly say that I had not had a taste for truth, and consequently no appetite for it, until it 'happened for me' in terms of poetry. And along with realizing a little bit what had been bothering me for a long time I also gained some immediate satisfaction, and this, I believe, had to do with a great hope reviving in me, the hope of being genuine and valid.

I know this implies that I had given up hope, and in a way that is quite correct. I had felt, and suspected, at one time, as a child, like most everyone I have ever spoken to about it, that my 'being around' made sense in some way. Then gradually, through the years, I acquired the notion from somewhere that in order for my 'being around' to make sense, a definite effort on my part was required, and that without such an effort I 'meant' nothing and amounted to very little. The onus was on me to make something of myself and I became accustomed to thinking of myself in terms of success and failure. At the same time the gap alarmingly widened between the opinion others had of me as a success and my own opinion of myself as a failure. I performed certain conventional tricks and acquired a number of skills which earned me praise and left me increasingly dissatisfied. One or two of my acquaintances who had arrived at a similar state of affairs decided they had hitherto espoused wrong values and they took sides with those who praised them, against their own dissatisfactions, and I noticed how smoothly it worked for them once they had taken the first step in that direction. A broad sense of approval enveloped them and in no time at all they looked down on me, in my sorry, mixed up state, and their eyes expressed feelings of pity and mockery. And right away there was mutual distrust. I think life had become rather easy for them suddenly and I had the distinct impression they would have preferred me out of their way because I compromised and embarrassed them, merely by being around. They had found their niche, as they called it; it was a fashionable expression at the time. I must have looked envious .

*

These are the times when I wish I could
carry the treasure entrusted to me
but the cold highway, the wet ditch,
still lively in my memory, shock me,
so I bow my head gladly, to see
what will happen if I rest here.

Why has no one seen fit to make these
natural kings, seated by the wayside,
actual kings too? It would only take
an insistence on favour, an underground
current of gratitude. Me, I have
terminated the luxuries of dying.

A tool in the right hand makes world
spring from the soil like daffodils
and the care you take when you operate
leads you into or out of the brushwood,
a singular occurrence notwithstanding,
and you sleep near the railroad track.

My feeble efforts at world dominion
were blown over by a child's smile.
The contagion of sexual frost set in
and shook the early snow from the trees,

from pine torn by a cold sea wind
where now the dancing has ceased.

But soon the dancing will begin again
and I have no doubt the superior music
will strike terror in the enemy's heart
and here the bountiful garden blooms
now in anticipation, seeming excitement,
so realize I know how to wait!

*

3

I am trying to give an impression of the truth here and by describing my experience of truth as a very young and impressionable person I am able to recall how I felt rather rebellious at times when people praised me for quite disrespectful performances and had no time at all for what I considered to be genuine contributions. The belligerence in me was aroused when it was suggested to me that only one further thing was required to make these responsibilities of mine quite perfect, and that was to surround them with an air of the prodigious. It dawned on me what it meant to foster charisma. What counted, so it was intended I should believe, was not so much what I did but rather how I presented it and how I tricked it out. The word truth wasn't used a great deal but I think the overriding temptation for me lay in a direction opposite to what I myself took for truth. Nobody, but nobody else agreed with me on that. Rather remarkable, really, until one learns later on, that it can lie in the very nature of truth for some of us to be singularly affected like this, to be gradually made aware of how part of 'me', the main part maybe, is like nobody and nothing else on earth but rather quite singular and unique – and how indeed we should have cause to worry if it were otherwise.

This realization amounts to a great deal and can make the difference between mental illness and sanity. A person with temperament, who hasn't been sickened by religious bigotry, might like to discover that God loves him as he is and that he does not first have to produce some sign of suitability. Popularity, in other words, is no way to mean what we say.

The fact that a few of us experience a desire or a strong logical need to act on this realization, from it and out of it, doesn't take away from the perfect value of the realization itself, of it as an end in itself even. Nobody can be convinced of such an insight, remain convinced of it, and not automatically have a salutary effect on his or her environment. And I don't want to move ahead too quickly here. My own personal experience with poetry will have to serve again, for the purpose of example and illustration.

4

*

Singing of itself has a use
when the singular mind
opens its heart to the light
and sound pours in
to settle where need dictates
or love makes a wish,
proving to all who would know
the vital requirements
of a happiness that lasts,
some pleasure taken
in giving oneself as voice,
some in the sober
welcome afforded.

Singing draws spirit down
and woos in effect
the lovely homecoming.
It cannot but anger
the typical, temporal bride,
fixed with a moral eye
to her own smooth skin's
self-evident fragrance,
for she hates confusion
such as the song is,
distinct from the singular
singer crowned by the song.

Ah, it sighs in me now
for the want of illusion,
this perfect image of song.
I recline beside her.
She cannot see me.
Wait, don't touch her,
but sing, if you would,
on her limbs with your fingers.

The moment you notice her move,
remain yourself unmoved,
return the well-being.

I make no amends
for the peace disturbed
or the silence broken.
Only the language itself
of the song in the singing
offers distinction.
The beloved body of the song
breathes in unison with the singer
and her breath invites
the lure of an endless kiss,
endless because unintentional,
truthful to blind the heart's
opposition to seeing.

The hard facts escape us.
Nevertheless the song
rises and falls.
She desires to blend in
with light lured from below.
She taxes the mindless eye,
operates in an untoward sweetness
too strong for compliance,
checks gently, chides with tongue
used to song, slowly
helps to facilitate
briefly the sound insertion.

Song sings itself sweetly
even in matter of fact voice
and the terrible dreaming
would not interfere with
the goalless intrusion of

that which would be
truly intruded.
That nothing should alter
the nude, tranquil encounter
of master and music,
muse and amusement,
luxury, laughter and pleasure,

in ease composed,

this orderly sphere of delights,
tender in passion, trans-
lates to a higher zone
and the song sings itself still
while she presents her breasts
to the searching mouth,
her mouth to the ear for
pure meaning spoken
and nothing eludes those
sensuous arms embracing
every which way, nothing
deludes those legs in their stride.

I am not content with
the song's system within, therefore
now make the melody wilder,
the nerve of note upon note of joy
sounder, wreck the rule of chance
by entering Lesbos more quietly,
where more than one instrument
perpetrates the love of examination.
You die here repeatedly
where no need to die exists,
considering how the brain sings
equally well in absentia,

or how the tide follows

more readily in train of the moon
once she has bathed there,
where the liquid singing around her
flatters her skin's brightness
with impish reflection,
while perfect sensations
filter through fingertips
the trembling lips.

Goodness stems from the song's
physical findings.
We who have paid
rapt attention a while,
letting the lyric disabuse itself
of some traditional vestiges
gathered while sex still maimed
the marital union of
voice and invested love,
exclaimed bitterly when the pain
brought by the word's procreation
threatened control.

But here the birth of song,
of new song from love's womb,
forced the revolution erotic,
freed the pale ghost of
uncalled-for enterprise,
raised the corrupt corpse,
long thought past healing,
from passages underground
and carefully imposed
an infinite ordering,
truthful sensations in harvest,
steadfast in rendering.

*

I can remember the first time a poem made a real difference to me, in the sense that I was given a glimpse of the power contained there, and I experienced it as shock, because rather suddenly my entire human nature was affected. I closed the book quickly, full of a terrible sense of dread. 'What in heaven's name is this!' was what I felt, and: 'Careful, this is s till too big for you!' I think I could compare it favourably to a sudden discovery of high voltage, and a forced appreciation of my own ignorance with respect to the proper and safe wiring of a circuit. It was a poem written in the thirteenth century, by the way, and I was especially startled by the fact that something with such a slick externality and such a playful manner could pack such an uncanny punch. My relative unfamiliarity with the personal medium, the cultural idiom and the historic setting had, I dare say, much, if not most, to do with the intense abruptness of the experience, but I must admit that if I had wanted to arouse both the curiosity and the respect of someone of my particular temperament I couldn't have come up with a better way of doing it. I opened the book again right away and took another peek, more careful, less unaware this time. It lay in front of me all innocent there, the poem on the page, and it smiled, I insist it did, and said: Got you.

Until then I had more or less been toying with the notion of poetry. One had read, one had studied and talked about it. Now these things began to take a more serious turn for me. Here, after all, was something worth doing – I thought about it like that – something so obviously for me to do; and no one else could do it, and unless I did it, it would remain undone. As far as my feeling was concerned, the energy and the force and the power were what counted. I preferred strength to weakness, and this poetry smacked of strength, if I may put it that way. With respect to my thinking on the other hand, well, that was where truth as such came into it in my case. I learned about truth before it occurred to me to wonder about 'the truth'. At the moment I don't want to make too much of the distinction, however due entirely to poetry, I would say, I regained my interest in such matters as meaning, purpose and value of life, trite enough propositions when viewed in detachment from the questionable security of the coffin but of vital concern to the adolescent who hasn't yet given up the ghost.

Now I ought to mention here that truth, for my sake at the time, seemed first of all to point to something which I later on called wisdom, but I could not then and cannot now get away with calling it wisdom without right away drawing that well-rehearsed, though perhaps of late, in our time, not so well performed, distinction between the sage and the child. All too well endowed with a chemical predilection for the gigantic and a mechanical penchant for the monstrous, I soon learned to appreciate and to value little things and to esteem and cherish what was generically small. If only one of something existed I tended to take especial notice and if in addition it appeared neglected and was easily overlooked I had to take care so as not to identify with it entirely. In truth I discovered a kind of pattern for that sort of behaviour. Poetry allowed me to consolidate that pattern and even seemed to encourage me to go beyond it, to finish it in some sense, as though it were strangely up to me to draw one or two final conclusions with respect to the infinite. I don't suppose anyone with a sense of mission in his youth will misunderstand what I mean. At the same time, as I think back on it now, I can enjoy a happy and hearty laugh. What is it about truth anyway that makes some of us want to break out in goose bumps and giggle at the same time? I cannot for the life of me see my way clear to apologizing for it. Truth is such a dry word. A good friend of mine once told me: To hell with your truth; what interests me is beauty! – and that remark still puts me in stitches. But in all fairness, I think I know well enough what he meant. He did not want me to preach. He wanted to be shown. And I reckon when poetry sets out to preach truth it should either take care to fit itself into a very tight aesthetic category, or else it should admit it was only fooling, drop the mask and stand revealed as politics. Truth and politics, in my books, avoid each other like the plague, which does not imply, by the way, that politicians are liars, but rather that truth just simply doesn't enter into it. Well, maybe.

10

But let me follow up this notion of the truthful pattern:

When lovers meet, when lovers greet,
I mean the usual, ritual way,
(we know it well enough from Art)
and some of them are free to love,
while others cling to iron bars
set there by will and circumstance –

when lovers meet and greet like this,
don't we all like to wish them well,
within the law, without the law,
hopefully not against the law,
and may the homes their spirits leave
remind them of the home they find.

Not so in one case I have heard
just recently by word of mouth.
The world, as I implied above
ten lines ago, takes irony
to be its lawful wedded bride
and neither you nor I can help it.

These lovers met and then they wed
one night beneath the glowing moon
and both were young as young can be,
sweet Jenny, sixteen, tall and dark,
the darling of the high school play,
high forehead and a sensuous mouth,

proud bearing, but of temper mild
and in her eye that lively spark
that first attracted Michael's eye
when one day, on the way from town
she stopped and waited for him there,
you know, where now the railway bridge

stretches across the Old Clay Road
with bramble on the left and right
so thick it would ensnare a hind.
Michael walked with her a spell
and as they talked it seemed as though
each knew the other's secret thoughts.

They played no thought-provoking games,
no tests of courtship seemed required
and in each other's arms that night
they lay and whispered words of trust
while overhead the bombers cruised
on missions of a different nature.

The wedding on a summer's night
took place beneath the glowing moon
and Michael wondered how it came
that premonitions in his heart
of sombre mood and sickening dread
disturbed him all that summer's night

as open-eyed he stared perplexed
at crumpled sheets and whitewashed walls
while naked Jenny seemed to him
a thing mechanical and wild
and distant as the traffic noise
beneath the window on the street.

And Jenny? She obeyed the laws
of her conventional routine
absorbed from movies on the screen
and from the glossy magazine,
but useful knowledge she had none
as ears had heard or eyes had seen.

What mysteries of the sexual bloom
of life lay hidden from the gaze
to be discovered and reviewed
in unison with her beloved,
what pleasures tasted, sweet delights
absorbed into the thinking heart:

of these they neither knew nor cared,
so trapped in ignorance were they,
by false opinion, bad report,
the broadcasts of commercial minds
on profit bent, devoid of worth,
and little faith they had in god

which turns all lonely pain to good.
During the next ten years they lived
in rented house from hand to mouth
and brought five children to the world
for whom they slaved obediently
with one eye on the rights of man

and one on happiness, which fled
before them like a frightened bird
that lures the fox to save its young.
Then Jenny acquiesced to things
and hoped no more for peace of mind

but she resorted to a drug
that promised to impair the brain
in such a way that nothing sad
could penetrate her conscious mind
and this was called by many work
while others called it cowardice.

And Michael, with his hands so full
of matters that pertained to death,
seemed predisposed, by guilt and shame,
to what his mother once had called
the idle speculations of
the curious flesh, and had maintained

an icy silence of the sort
too hateful to deserve respect,
but not too weak to generate
reaction in man's later life,
when cause and motive long lie dead
and precepts are entombed in dreams.

That was a metaphysical
aside and I apologize.
I should have started to relate
how one day Michael drove to work
and there beside her jacked-up car
he spied the lovely Christabel

struggling with a punctured tyre.
She couldn't get the wheel-nuts off
the studs, the wrench slipped, she hurt
her hand. He stopped and rolled the window down and spoke to her like this:

'Oh Christabel, dear Christabel,
I see things aren't going well
for you; oh dear, you've hurt your hand,
I'd better give you one, alright?
Hold everything, I'll park the car
ahead and help you with that wheel.'

All philosophical asides
aside, that's how your mischief starts.
If Christabel had waved him on
or said: no thank you, I can manage,
she would have been a liar, and worse,
a little stupid, don't you think?

While Michael, fired by chivalry,
(or so he thought) had long since lost
the knack for the impartial deed;
and so he stooped, then she stooped too,
in contemplation of the tyre –
her hair touched his, their fate was sealed.

When love strikes home like this, it makes
no difference what we do or say.
Your prudent maxims, learned by rote,
must fail, since love will have its way.
So love some more, don't fight the thing
or hate will make your hair turn grey.

Now Michael, for some months, spent hours
with Christabel each afternoon
discussing work, discussing life,
(they were both in the insurance business)
and gradually what they fondly called
their mutual understanding grew.

While Jenny, 'happy in her work',
(the drug was working, she complied;
she managed a department store)
thought Michael, too, seemed more content,
less quarrelsome; the children too –
one hardly noticed how they grew.

It was the lull before the storm.
A practiced eye predicts these times,
does violence to the slothful heart
before that vicious fiend can rise
and full of vengeance, malice, lies,
tear body, soul and brain apart.

The next event still makes me cringe,
it goes so much against my grain.
It's as if nature sometimes could
give up all claims to right and law
and choose a path that seems to us
against itself, in short: perverse.

But I suspect that we're to blame,
not nature, human or divine.
We stand so far back from ourselves,
especially when we're feeling fine,
that we mistake the love we make
for signs of the returning life.

But when the life returns and when
the truth comes back again to us,
or put it this way, when the word
reclaims its long neglected sphere
of action, and the way is free
to song and dance for you and me,

or suddenly the light divides
the night and moves in giant strides
across the earth's abused terrain
to bring all things to light again
as happens now, in what we call
our own time when we give our all,

when all this happens – there's no sign
and while we see signs it's not here.
Demands for evidence and proof
mean that the brain remains aloof,
so that when Mike brought 'Christa' home
should Jennifer not have hit the roof?

Please, Jenny, Mike said, don't be vexed.
You know how much this concept covers:
she's under-sexed, I'm over-sexed,
in short, the two of us are lovers.
We didn't want to keep you guessing,
and so we came here for your blessing.

Was Jenny stunned? I'll say she was.
Her face went paler than this paper.
One struggles, one suspends belief:
is this an adolescent caper?
I'd rather not say how she felt;
with all this art, your heart would melt.

She sank down on a kitchen chair,
so speechless you could hear her thinking.
Her hands were buried in her hair
and then she heard the glasses clinking.
They had poured themselves a gin and tonic.
Their eyes lit up and gleamed demonic.

In her numb state Jenny asked questions
as though the milkman had confronted her.
Transported into a state of fiction
she felt she ought to follow rules,
be polite, conventional in her responses,
though she couldn't ignore their secret glances.

'So what do you expect me to do?'
'Could you not tell us you don't hate us?'
'What? Hate? No, I don't hate you. Why?'
'You won't make a scene?' 'No, why should I?'
'Ah Jenny, you're a friend in need.
Isn't she, darling. So understanding.'

Apparently this went on for weeks,
that Jenny tried to make some sense
of these rather novel circumstances.
The man in her house came home from work
and praised his girl, excused his lateness,
she had kept him, needed his support.

Did her husband want to be her son?
What was she? Sister? Mother? Wife?
Whose wife? Her own son looked attractive.
Why, even Christabel's broad shoulders
gave Jenny a kind of strange thrill
and she experienced loathing for her daughter.

Then one day something inside her snapped.
He had passed the cornflakes absentmindedly.
For once her mood required no staging:
she raged and got her fill of raging.
A little stunned, he sat in silence
and waited until the storm blew over.

The way he sat there, stuffed with reason,
let Jenny know her life had altered.
The way her rage had left her twisted,
let Michael know his life had changed.
The children's chorus had borne witness:
no family was left worth saving.

When truth is long enough neglected,
what seems like love, by death inspected,
breaks down; the conscience is infected
and unless our mind is resurrected
in him to whom the Jews objected
while Christians on his death reflected,

all comes to nought in single figures
and fades from sight, from touch and hearing.
The individual atom sniggers
while bare existence starts appearing
and man of woman born engenders
the death to which his flesh surrenders.

*

But truth is nothing if not formal. A truthful pattern magnifies the truth for us, and this magnification stimulates life. It may even stimulate life in such a way that it proves stronger than death and when such life finds itself out through poetry, we are participating in the finest poetry of all. One might say that it facilitates the path from truth to the truth and then on to reality.

Truth, at the beginning, is simply accepted as an aspect of nature. To make something out of it, to give it shape, this requires its contemplation by a gifted mind and we should take care to remember that a gifted mind, in the way I want to make use of the term here, is not in itself and automatically of benefit to anyone, unless that gift is accepted. Reject the gift long enough, or let it lie unapplied, and it turns into a curse. So many human beings are adversely affected by what, in truth, are benefits for them and our heart goes out to them because their miserable state could so easily be rectified if they were to use the various forces already with- in their natural power to their proper end. Poetry can demonstrate the proper and germane application of these forces even as it intrigues the lesser capacities of the mind or of the body and seduces them into a recognition of their inferiority to superior states of being.

Patterns of truth we come across where we find them and they appeal to us one at a time. We know truth wherever we initiate our knowledge and from the very point of its departure but the pattern is supplied to it by the necessity of some particular moment with which we comply. Our compliance, and our willingness to continue to be compliant for a time, under whatever circumstances, should offer itself to our notice during that time; this is what renders the truthful pattern fruitful.

The poetic experience, the reading or writing of a poem, should therefore first of all teach the wisdom of such a compliance, basically of an inferior with a superior form of life. The right wisdom shows how to differentiate between, on one hand, inferiority and superiority, and on the other hand moral inferiority and superiority. If the relationship is moral, it is entered into under someone's eyes, in the company, real or imagined, of some third party and consequently, instead of becoming life-productive and vital towards an end – it will become death-reactive while cloaked in superstitions of immortality. If the relationship of inferiority-superiority is not moral but express and clear it facilitates an emotional contribution and a compassionate investment of our human nature as such, within some lively frame of reference, in a live manner.

The singularity of every pattern of truth constitutes a law unto itself:

> Were I a man of noble mind,
> not driven to sacrifice by the lords of time
> who will exist as long as time exists
> and they march under the banner of
> love of fortitude and administration –
>
> were I such a man as
> speaks his mind on all manner of things,
> lukewarm towards the messianic ideals
> but callous when it comes to
> strife for the sake of mere gain:

then no one should bind me.
No house should hold me unless
the crude lettering on the walls
had been carefully removed, the base
intention exorcised from the brick.

Look how the spirit holds me
calmly in milk-white hand, how
the viciousness of the legislators
cannot harm me, but only the
doublet protects me from false reason.

By the absolute god who dwells in tents
I swear not, his robe I tear not,
yet it exasperates my patience how he
looks on while his disciples die
and bring no weak thing to fruition.

Know therefore, as years pass by,
and the doll-queen rages against elements,
that an ambassador has arrived,
has thatched his cottage with impunity,
has carried the work forward to its conclusion.

But an empty brain with a
stone for a heart in it cannot safely
cross borders where the wolves raid
nightly the wagon train, and an image
rests, curiously attired, were I sleep.

Grow, death-devouring majesty,
in among clouds and around them,
for no one provokes, no one tempers
the right honourable facility of what
slaves once called Christ and survived.

I am not hated by the nations,
my foolishness tests no leaders of men,
Tiberius would find me blameless,
so without rancour, standing alone,
will my spirit remain tireless.

Nothing requests life so much
as the impoverished eagle in its
proscribed wisdom, relegated
by the world's pre-nuptial acrobats,
whose sides my spear finds.

And when you curse the fact that a hart
has escaped and the hunt runs blind,
think instead of a settled
existence behind enemy lines
and how sweet revenge would taste then!

I am an absent-minded lodger,
disputing the rook's nest of a night
riddled by the wild birds' cries
and my reason would involve me in love
where eventually my flesh begets joy.

*

Since no one can say beforehand how he is going to be affected
by any instance of poetic truth, we can put our mind at rest. Consequently, it seems, we can say in addition that no one can know how
he is being affected by poetic truth while he exists under its influence.

An affect plagues us until we give in to it and then knowledge can
get to work on it. The irritation of affects needs to be interpreted.
Their challenge presents us with the opportunity for progress and
growth.

The best way to meet the challenge of an affective magnitude is usually, in my own experience at least, head on. I find that while I try to negotiate, I lose credibility fast. So it would seem to take less brain than courage, to bend to the task with a will.

Now probably most anyone who has ever seen fit to make an independent effort at freedom can testify to the experience of anguish, and it will have occurred to him that there must be a better response to it, in the long run if not in the short term, than revolt. He can shake off the weight and the bother of it for the moment and pile it on someone else, but it does return, is that not so? In fact I have observed it returns nearly twice as affectively – if we are so fortunate. A louder knock would attract our attention where the gentler one failed.

It helps, of course, to be able to break down anguish into physical and emotional affects, when our intellect gets busy as though it knew what it were doing, however here we have to take care that the intellect remains as a tool in our hands, else it loses itself.

Anguish, or the fear of something that would do us good, becomes a prime target for the poetic intellect, which is to say: the intellect trained towards poetry. It is a delusion when we believe we might take an interest in what causes the anguish. As soon as we face it, we realize that some shortcoming in ourselves has caused it and that the affect points us in the direction of perfection.

The nutritional aspect of the poetic intellect I dealt with in a companion piece to this one; I only want to repeat the caution here: While we can give a name to something we ought to do so, not out of a need for locking ourselves into a brain-tight sphere of identical meaning but so that we can be cured of any and every fear, whatever the origin. What we call something is crucial but that we call it something in the first place is imperative. This in itself has for some become cause for apprehension. They would be freed of any need for universality and so they look to each other for solace in agreement. This avoids the truth and destroys the pattern of truth.

Pattern as such is part of what we call truth anyhow. It manifests itself in appearances. Our environment gives evidence of it in detail. Each and every detail of our environment bears testimony to the singularity of the pattern in every case. Just as the number of things around us is infinite – which is why we count any number of them in the first place – so are the multiplicity and variety of pattern. Some poets manage to point this out and make it more clear, more legitimately credible, to others.

Due to the diversity of pattern in the appearance of things, and due to this diversity being endless, truth is shown forth and becomes demonstrable. The monotony and boredom of existence, the mere repetition of resemblances and so on, is therefore simply to be lifted by the demonstration of truth in the pattern of things around us.

Poetry demonstrates truth, and this is a good thing, because it recovers the source of our vitality. Vitality is normal, but fatigue, exhaustion, laxness and slackness, tiredness etc., these are not normal, but they point affectively to a demonstration of truth:

> The miracle of a clear day
> makes all manner of thing fine.
> The calm curiosity of a bird,
> matter of fact for a while,
> signals an element of love.

> Where the child trusts his mind
> to magnify the sun's illumination
> and morning to evening overshadows
> the blaze of an innocent heart,
> there too the spirit flowers.

> Being idle among the intent crowds,
> a child slips from his mother's hand
> and right away doors close softly
> on the parish of deserved freedom,
> a mist to mystify the eye.

Sadly the children dance
around the death of their childhood,
buried beneath the rockslide,
and this illustration of sorrow
also fills in the day.

Angels close their ears
to the wailing of the children, inclining
instead to the roar of the rockets,
tender in their compassion,
but unable to reach children.

Why do they not bury their
spirits where the train rumbles
across the self-same continent as
Darius surveyed on his tripod
or Catullus dreamt into a sphere?

Nothing may weary the sailor
once he has accepted the past,
ponderous beneath sea foam,
or his memory of home holds
surprises he has dared to face.

I am sailor, child, mountaineer,
trapped by needless pain under
infinite comparisons, objective
nevertheless, and my keen eye
fits these pains to the times.

*

The demonstration of truth for the sake of vitality centres on
our affective nature. We need to clarify what we mean by our affective nature, otherwise we shall not be able to cope with it.

Affective is that which forces itself on our attention and it reacts
to any authentic appeal or genuine concern, whereas it responds to
the imposition of limits and the composition of its elements.

The way it reacts, when it does, causes distress and leads to an overwhelming experience. This should be avoided by poetry. There can be no profit in sowing the wind.

The way it responds, however, must be of critical interest to us, because here we come face to face with the raw materials of music and the stuff that goes most legitimately into the make-up of drama.

Poetry knows very well how to travel in the guise of music and how to act the part of drama. Dramatic poetry and musical poetry, not categories or genres, but species of poetry, are therefore, logically considered, the true birthplaces and homes of poetic genius:

> Where it goes, what it does,
> always makes men alert,
> women brave, children cheerful
> beyond mere bounds on hallowed grounds
> and let no one stand in its way.

> You have tortured me enough, love,
> and look, I'm happier than ever.
> Not what you expected, I dare say,
> when you called my name in the city
> and hunted me from private rooms.
> Of course I had made a name for myself
> but those who knew carefully forgot
> so that from the simplicity of my last refuge
> I came forth spectral and haunted the alleyways,
> lifted my hand against the beast within,
> struggled uphill to admire the ungainly
> advantages of tradition and culture –
> only to be swept away by this stream
> which burst all convention asunder.

> Then I waited at the iron gate,
> content to wait, cool in the moonlight.
> Snowflakes whirled past the face of the

image set up in stone there to frighten the traveller,
and I too sensed danger, doubled my watch.
Things made by man tend to accumulate,
to rear up beneath triumphal arches
irrespective of one's capacity for trial.

When the gate opened to the blast of trumpets,
light poured like gold from within.
Deafened and blinded, seized by anxiety,
I clung to a horse's bridle, was dragged
by the knowledgeable incarnation of a god
through the gate, past armies of darkness.

Now I look back on my experiences out there
with a forgiving eye and I trace the pattern
of this traumatic arrival on wings of violence
in steel and glass, on gold and marble.

Don't think it doesn't occur to me
to run people's lives for them,
to make them see the light:
the height of vain stupidity –

since all manner of worthwhile persuasion
has to deal in freedom, work through freedom,
built into the clock, pronounced by angels.

No more can I cause the sensation of a man
than god can deny himself universal satisfaction,
though groan in sickness may the world
or writhe in anguish on the nuptial couch,
oh citizens of sustained self-will and home cooking.

*

Drama is the treatment of our affective nature with the view of
rendering it wholesome, whereas music is the leading out of our affective nature for the purpose of our own soundness in body and
mind.

Poetry, then, is dramatic when it applies itself affectively and musical when it educates affectively. Once we have isolated an affect, for example, such as gravity in my present case, we can hope for some gain for recognizing it as such. We can penetrate any reaction to it on our part by rendering the affect conceptual, can trust the affect, eventually to become fundamentally objective, can support and maintain a subjective respectability in view of the affect, can learn how to cope under the influence of the affect without trying to manipulate some imaginary cause of it, can suffer any discomforts or inconveniences that come along with this, can feel the affect as continuously and constantly as possible and let it make a difference to our distinct imagination, can express this difference in the interest not of anything described but of a record kept, of signs posted as it were, for the sake of an advance into unknown territory and permanent settlement there. Empirical wisdom is of the essence. We act out each and every experience as it comes along, not bothering to abstract from it but refraining from adding to it, and in this business of acting out the momentary experience lies the secret of dramatic success, poetic to the extent of its investment in the heart's own language:

> The political situation on this island
> fills me with trepidation.
> Extreme points of view are being held
> and intolerant opinions are voiced,
> which leads to disenchantment.
>
> Should I not also perhaps
> show some muscle, carry some weight,
> root around in my innards and make
> a sensible contribution to peace?
>
> Look at these emotions for example,
> the rage that builds up when I hear
> self-complacency chattering next door,
> the difficulty I have with forgiving
> a single person her individual style.

It hurts so much when my flesh acts
up as though it knew a thing or two,
that a murderer takes shape in me.
I do not think he will listen to policies.
Nothing accommodates him except
an occasion for blood-letting and strife.

What a shame that I cannot create
a climate around myself of soft kindness,
an atmosphere of sublime open-mindedness
as though stars poured straight into my brain.
Then I would risk a political speech or two.

But of course I know what I should do is
stick to my last and not cast aspersion on
those who strive to modify the times,
preaching like others their own humanity.

Trouble overshadows me soon enough
and I hasten to make an example of it
or of myself accused by circumstances.

'Law and order are under political control'
a gentleman suggests on Question Time.

*

While dramatic poetry makes exacting demands on our constitution, musical poetry lets us know what we appreciate while we appreciate it:

A note of confidence

But we were promised
so much, such powers and
pleasures and beauty, that
in anticipation impatience makes
our hearts fail, our brains falter
and I stand like a child, thumb in mouth,
waiting for Mummy to fix it.

And she does, bless my soul,
who would have thought it! She
scoops me up in her arms, not at
all allegorical, but concentrating on
me only for a moment, in spite of
that selfish streak down my back.

So, I admit it, I am shamed
into better deeds. I make allowances now
for the ups and downs of the earth's
startling topography, and in woods
I willingly accept rest.

This has caused me disquiet:
the way the streets move away from me,
and my next of kin can no longer
recognize me, so it seems.

All of us ought to be able to
celebrate the fact that we exist and
then call that celebration life.

Instead I dimly suspect I shall
soon wake up and have nothing
to eat, no bed to sleep in, only self-
recrimination and perhaps charity.

Ordinarily I pretend to like these stones,
these metal parts hinged each to each
by some industrious brother's foresight,
but today the excessive sunlight confuses me
and I may seek aid, from vegetation.

But drugs only stimulate or distress
my less than original dissatisfaction with
the millpond, where my son drowned,
the legendary bird that stole
my father's sex, the crude reflections
under which my country cannot bear up.

But sing, and a new world opens,
so that all these shadows, now clinging,
spring into a life so rare and fortuitous
that only an extended surprise can
illustrate my meaning when I say:
Come to your senses, make an end of
this particular joy and start the next.

*

It doesn't matter much that we can read these poems without a
sidelong glance at anything else we have ever read if we don't at the
same time come to some conclusion about the value of affective experience, for ourselves mostly, I suppose, and we ought to ask ourselves in all seriousness: How long has it been now since we have
stopped mocking irrational behaviour in others because it makes us
feel uncomfortable? And when exactly did we decide to let someone
else's point of view count for us even though it goes strictly against
our grain?

The subject matter of these poems is not intended to take us in,
but if it does, a guarantee is built into the poem so that no one, of
whatever persuasion, can come to any harm. We contain such a guarantee in our own make-up, and we would rely on it if we knew it. Because we think we take fantastic chances, when in truth we couldn't be
more secure.

When poetry makes it its task to demonstrate this guarantee
against injury in our make-up, it invites us to concern ourselves, in all
dignity and good taste, with ostensibly disparate elements, with super-
ficially unrelated types of complication, with the commonplace in eso-

31

teric use and the personal secret paraded openly as metaphor. The thread of continuity demanded by the analytical understanding may be tied into all sorts of knots, diversion and digression may abound, and all that matters is that our heart is in the right place. Language has to create a context so that the position of the heart, its truthful location, may be ascertained. If some one particular faculty holds the monopoly on what we're about, then that faculty will draw attention to itself and become a nuisance, while truth is cast back.

Another worthwhile ambition is that of the peacemaker. He points out misunderstanding, but mostly to himself, because he knows how due to our affective fixations we refuse to have the form of our understanding manipulated or changed. So once he has spotted the misunderstanding, he decides on a gap there, room which he makes for himself on account of what he saw out there, and then he creates a substitute experience, a vehicle for transition, so that opponents can meet in terms of it without losing face and impressed by a degree of immediate freedom.

The peacemaker draws on truth to help him stay within the bounds of the practical. Without it he moralizes, preaches loftiness and urges sublimity. We recognize him by the way he waits until he has heard all three sides of the story before he speaks, and then mostly not to judge or to upbraid, nor to fix blame, but to let himself be used as a servant by those who would insist on tyranny. He reflects before he speaks and he considers before he acts, and when he does anything he realizes that he has done it.

Poetry that draws on truth to this end has exactly the same use. It makes tranquil within us the warring factions that have lost control of their purpose. It eases the corrupt faculties where neglect has pushed them beyond the bounds of conscience. It comforts the distraught nerves and blandishes the inflamed temper where error and wrongdoing have hardened attitudes and ingrained bad habits. And then finally it offers a position of freedom from where truth may be chosen, where it may be seen and even where it exists:

There's nothing wrong with me.
I threw a stone into the pond
and no concentric ripples appeared.
I am merely out of fashion.

From the Rocky Mountains to the Chinese Wall
a million illuminations herald the homecoming
of him whose terror fixed the stars
and he knows himself in each blade of grass.

Only those who live the eternal life
can find a proper end to things
such as rain out of a cloudless sky
or a swan dancing before the wind.

Suddenly to be stretched out in one's
spoiled feebleness like a canvas to the
hard, harsh wintry earth and naked sky
makes for a quick recognition of proportions.

Perhaps it is too cold yet to reach out and
strike beauty from the living branch.
When the jangle of skylark strikes terror
into the convenient heart, though tears
promise release, and mallard on the pond
hate for courtship's sake, ask yourself:
of what use is it to hold out? But do
not ask too seriously, for your answer will
lack proportion, will falsify, under pressure,
the simple fit of things called truth.

The way the wind curls the pond towards me,
away from that dark line at the far shore,
teaches the central marrow of my bone
and while part of all of us craves sunshine,
when after weeks of wet and cold we shiver,
exposed to our authentic existence in time,

we nevertheless would involve a demonstration
of security in despite, of measured appreciation,
even while all around blind forces gulp
ill prepared bodies of flesh down whole
and call it the exercise of domestic science.

*

To feel the truth while we give expression to it is a special blessing. We have an unfailing guide then as we pursue our activity and
we soon learn to confine ourselves to such moments of experience as
do not interfere with our life but usher it in and see it out, as we
give of our life or gain more. The exchange of life, which is called
abundant life or life in abundance, can be poetically exemplified so
that we reside in truth even as we deal with the life due to that residence in a manner befitting our time and place. But eternal life in
contemporary garb moves as it is moved, changes as it is changed, by
the very necessity of lived life as such, which is to say not of life as a
concept or an illustration but as our reason for existence in the first
place. If we were to speak of a spirit of life, therefore, we would also
have to speak 'as' a spirit of life, in order to make sense, I mean,
rather than hypocrites of ourselves. And this is usually difficult precisely because it is so free and easy and because all of our faculties
are supposed to deny themselves, all our learned techniques and acquired skills and derived wisdom are supposed to put themselves
wholly at the service of the one, which is that it is, recognizable by the
fact of our total visual assimilation in face of it, knowable by the attributes it allows us to apply to it in truth, understandable insofar as
we insist on being one with it, and so on.

Poetry which bears witness, by example, to the one in all, may
be called transcendental poetry, and it is the simplest of all, the most
open and readily available, the finest and greatest. Its most character-
istic application measures for us our distance from ourselves, our estrangement from our human nature, our adequacy when it comes to
the personality we have chosen over the personality we had acquired
or achieved. And along with such a measurement it supplies the

34

means whereby we may alter the size of what was measured if we so desire.

Out there green acres roll,
in here the bells toll
for the correction of a wasted life.
The blasted hopes and dreams,
once boyhood's buoyant joy,
are swept like fragments of stone and glass
away, out of mind's eye, away,
not to make scold the bilious priest
or rile the bachelor aunt.

A last hint of faded gold still gives
the vaguest outline of the western hills
where treachery sleeps, and a little woman
weeps herself out of misery a while,
not so excited by your excuses as
one might have hoped, considering the lust
for living bred within her.

Then back into this pretty crowded room
filled to the brim with furniture
like many a room, perhaps yours too,
and to make this room endless
by the application of spirit on mind, mind
on things, things on their images.

You too, whatever else you do during
the waking hours of an average day,
have what it takes to channel impotence
into the inner sanctum of power.
You too may drive the violence of your sex
like a wedge into the log of your heart and split
the ranks where the forces of evil sit,

and so, without making matters worse
or endangering the plight of man on earth,
you may join the banquet at the table,
its ends are always just out of sight,
except for those who must eat everything
before the smallest morsel is snatched away,
and time confuses them except in a straight line,
pictured as a wire from nail to nail –
you know best, Ambrose – immortal backbone.

The alter ego mentions what has occurred
in regions where eagles drink in sun.
In seventh heaven the glider loops the loop,
this is transferred onto film, and still
beauty chastens the mortal will,
spreads wings, threatens and protects
at once – the organism feigns sleep.

So that no tragedy with the harvest may interfere,
this area of most intense passion is
fenced round. You have come to your
wits' end here, my friend, make no mistake,
this is common human property,
communal real estate, you too have to
pass here, pass through or pass away,
I recognize that hang-dog expression,
the soured mien, the look of:
If I could care less I would – and yet
you amount to a phantom, an emptied space,
less than nothing, a negative individual,
unless you make some effort to plumb
your heart's desire, the fire in your loins,
unless you one time agree to take a trip
across that glacier in your brain that slides
between moraines of superstition and delusion

down towards the town for which your world stands
and look, how small by comparison!

*

What does amount to much more than I care for,
making a show of dignity and constraint,
of integrity and professional expertise – believe me,
the next one I know shall feel my hate – is that …
that… well, I described it just now.

Don't pretend you prefer to ignore it.
Let yourself get carried by it a distance,
and then
when it turns towards you
accusing you, worst of sins, of impoliteness,

smile and give a friendly nod of the head,
be not afraid, my friend, to act,
so as to tear out their liver, their throat.
Have you not put up long enough with their contempt?
Now you have the wherewithal at your disposal
to wreck their false imaginings with affection
and teach them the elegance of true high-mindedness.

Going out into the world
speak no other language
but drift with currents,
burn with straw
and give all manner of manner
your most musical conviction.

Lifting the lid from your box of tricks
you stand your ground, all innocent
and letting nature triumph over art,
believing even the outright lie.

You make amends for alleged error,
take down names where protocol requires,

fit plan to system, mind to eye
and refrain from all untoward indulgence.

This is a program, as you know,
and its simple instructions found their home
precisely where they ought; know only that,
and cultivate the single field of vision.

* *

The turmoil of the sea prevents the eye
from restful contemplation, and the sky
is filled with white birds, drifting gently
in gale force winds, each calculating eye
fixed at its root, hinged east and south

and that which was birds and sky and sea
has now become an integral part of me
that I may shift more wisely in the open,
with canny sense, steering a common course,
not perplexed by moods, amazed by mere force.

For we are given, with all our desires and lights,
the power to reach, to achieve and prosper,
be it rosebud dew-dropped or rocket hewn
from crystal brain-cells, sadly engineered
to endow a perfectly sufficient game with purpose.

In random shape lies eventual rest,
reprieve from chisel, pencil, rule.
The statue nature's child loves best
is worked with the eventual tool.

As time descends where earth lies prone
the flesh gives evidence of death
and nature speaks of coming norms
with each eventual dying breath.

Where gravity rises and gives shape

to the models of desire and hope,
there cosmic dust makes the mind escape
beyond those limits the fit hands grope.

Pencil, chisel, tongue and eye,
these force time from the mighty womb,
these give meaning without seeming,
seeming that depends on meaning,
duration in a living room.

Tendency to slight or squander,
thirst for where destruction takes us,
naked streets through towns whose shops
buy and sell the nation's tenure,
oh and when the music stops
who shall fetch and who shall carry,
who shall marry the girl in white,
her pretty flesh blown like dust –
how shall a man deceive her?

I am not supposed to tell this,
so I speak my mind about it:
The green hills frighten me so much,
the tragedy of the contemporary obsession
with the crude symbols of previous symbols
and these again filtered through a maze
which is in itself a symbol
of what? – I shall say anon.

Nameless heaven – tricky spinster,
warm in cushions none too ample,
predisposed to Fair Isle knitting
by a bloodline dedicated:
to love,
to murder and love,
to revenge, war and love,
to domination, hell and damnation,

oh, and love,
please, please do not forget love,
it excuses so much, it justifies the means,

being itself the transcendental end
to those poor minds who must
grovel in the historic dust
before they do what they would call transcend.

The virtual cradle of the virtuous world,
put together from sticks and staves
and smithied hoops and nails that rust,
still rocks away there and will for half a time yet;

which dates this letter, casts it beyond
the trivial ambitions and trivial hopes
of our better, improving, progressive self,
imagined as a bottle on a cupboard shelf,

magic the contents, of indeterminate origin,
The Tonic, you crave it, lust after it,
make it out to be or not to be something else,
which to the addict is all that matters.

Or by some miraculous predisposition
the fancied light of Hyperborean faith
gleams on dull topaz, glints on ice
so far north that no tears shall stream,
the remarkable efforts of people remaining
ever doubtful, thrust through with spears
of shame and spite and suspicion and
superstition, all nailed to a tree
and this then broadcast by the mass media.

What, does truth tire you?
How can that be?
Perhaps you have languished on sand
too long, have fixed your gaze

too narrowly on compromising gain
and now, when dreams possess you
and dictate the set of the jaw,
the pressure of thumbs against seams,
the fluid content of the emasculate eye,

only a whimper of dissension remains,
and that is all that is possible.

I would rather have drowned in tradition
under the weight of the millstone god
than to have harmed me when my time ripened.

These are troublesome times,
I know it as well as the next,
so consequently I make allowances
and include some dogma in my text:

* * *

Lord God, there are no cages left,
it's freedom or it's doom,
and poets round the campfires sit,
their backs to where the embers spit,
and stare into the gloom.

My love has borne for me such pain
as I am loath to say,
and yet I cast myself in doubt
or bring the death of love about,
and flee the light of day.

(and yet I cast myself in doubt
where angels weep and demons shout)

*

So the world laments its passing.
The grand view is vouchsafed me
across the earth's endless curve,

41

endless since it enters souls and minds
and as it dips out of recognition,
conjuring the image of a hand that
cherishes and holds all life dear,

it brings the hearts and lives more near
of those who, like children, crave
the inner contest, that most laudable game
played to amuse the gods we are,
sanctioned by the inferior spirits
searching within us for a goal,
an empty dream within which to reside.

So do hell's portals open wide
and out stream the rejected mortals,
eyelids torn back, mouths agape,
as though expecting yet another torture,
but nothing happens, only the result
of many bad years spent in isolation
insistent on knowledge, right and sight,

descends and overthrows them quite.
But they are helpless and they mutter
ephemeral maledictions, they blow curses
to each other with manners and style,
like plants perhaps, dipped by the wind
and caused to pollinate from without.

Away! Wipe this vision away! Trust only
in the cloudless perfection of the rose
and then accept both cloud and shade,
both the cloud and its shadow, speech
aboriginal from the cloud's quick centre
and then the rose, cast out, at the feet
of him who stands with feet on earth,

terrorizing the vast immortal hordes
who fled from death not into truth
nor yet into the light's seeming anguish,
(to an awful engendering predisposed),
but outward into image of themselves
preferring the popular histrionics
and the undead certainties of sere age.

It seems we are held down and back and in,
merely by fascination of this infernal din
and by the fear, the near transcendental fear,
that too few human beings live up here.

And those that do must trumpet out their shame
at general life's loss, as though it were a game
and they may not join hands or hearts for fear
that they will form a closed society up here.

They may not correspond in lively letters,
comparing agreement on ideas of a similar strain,
nor embrace in congregations, congenial in the flesh,
lest fear of freedom swallow up love's gain.

Never mind, dear children of the heroic spirit,
crushed salt of tilled earth, spring's promise of
first fruits, laughter amidships while the time's
timbers groan and creak, demonstrating strength –

through such as this work take sweet cognizance
of one another's presence on the earth's heavenly
nature reserve, in heaven's earthly domain
and let not those who separate real life make you

resentful, doubtful or in any way unsure,
use your own self to dull their hateful knife's
smiling edge, and smile right back, lovely to
look upon, letting no unkind thought enter.

'My province is the inner man',
the poet says and knows his place.

But why does he say that?
How does he come to say such a thing?

What about the engineer who says:
'I should like to enter heaven.'

Must we absolutely distinguish between
lesser mortals and lesser evils

and has our capacity for pure creativity
limits that are dictated from outside?

* * * *

I am a power-hungry Cyclops
seated on the steps to the Parthenon
and I let no one prescribe for me
my actions or justifications for them.

I make fish-eyes at Herodotus,
trapped in my own embarrassment
and now and again, when young girls pass,
I scratch ciphers into the sand.

This is no ordinary mutilation of
man's flesh I propose, as I set about
doing what I was born for, according to
my own lights and decisions, mind you.

I describe this as an act of authentic
mythology, because I fancy myself, and
because ordinary words are not good enough
to keep me from shaking myself down.

Oh, trust the historians to hack my
corpse to pieces as soon as they get their
moist hands on it, their grubby fingers,
so accustomed to the touch of corruption.

But I shall stand by in spirit,
one-eyed and drunk with power,
ready to drive them insane as soon as
they return to their wives and children.

* * * * *

Transcendental poetry, as we observed above, naturally comes round, once it has reached the apex of human understanding, to the production of myth. The transcendental process from a beginning to an end must precede before we can expect true myth, which is to say an illusion of contemporary magnitude rooted in truth.

The impact of myth is due to its abrupt creation within no context. We are suddenly confronted by it and fall into a relationship with it, any relationship at all.

The effect of myth is affective. It appeals to our moods, to our likes and dislikes, to our temperament and, last but not least, to our physical constitution. The nature of the appeal is forceful and powerful.

We can speak quite intelligently about the production of myth, and we may roundly call this mythology, but the production of a myth makes no sense at all. When the production of myth is subsumed in poetry, as in our case, rather than in painting, or prose, or music, which might equally well be the case, then we may draw out the comparison by saying that just as poetry includes the reader or writer of it, so does mythology imply a maker or a minder of it.

But let's keep in mind that mythology needs either poetry or prose or sculpture in order to be able to come out into the open as it were. We cannot say that it requires an art, or some other art, to lead it out, because that would imply that mythology is not an art or an art among others, which would be incorrect and misleading. So we have to be both particular and specific. And this in itself affords us a couple of important clues.

Making myth or minding it, they both come to the same, and we use the same terms to describe either. Making a myth on the other hand is tantamount to telling a lie. Adolf Hitler may supply a most recent and glaring example of a man responsible for making a myth, or several of them, if you care to look at it that way. And when you make myths you can count on the masses. While myth is rooted in the truth, myths are rooted in particular egos. In order to dislodge a myth from an ego we have to confront it with myth, and this succeeds because myth is powerful and potentially good, while myths are mighty, which is to say egotistical and potentially bad and false, so that the struggle between myth and myths boils down, in all individual cases, to a struggle between truth and falsehood.

'Minding myth', (not a colloquial usage but no neologism either), compares to 'reading poetry', when we are 'into it', working our way around in it, making use of it – but then all this applies to making poetry too while we are 'making myth'. (You notice how we have to stay close enough to make honest sense but far enough back to maintain both a sense of perspective and a sense of proportion. Both these senses are valuable in the task we have undertaken, basically a critique of creativity. Move in too close and we begin to talk popular nonsense but move away too far and get trapped in private rubbish. Usually then the private rubbish is mistaken for public property and the popular nonsense is mistaken for esoteric wisdom. However none of us can help that. The thing to do is to keep in touch without becoming possessive.)

The secondary attraction of myth has been mentioned, the way it needs poetry, for one example, to usher it into being. From the point of view of the creator one might call it delayed action. The creator, not either divine or human but both, anticipates the myth as a unique companion-piece to himself, for the sake, eventually, of what we can only call express logic. No one separates or divorces man from god in this, or either man or god from the world. We can say that god came first and created the world and man, because that was in the past; but right now, in the present, it makes no sense to say whether it is god creating man or man creating god, or who first creates the world with the other in it, because at the moment, in eternal time, we are 'all in all'.

Mythology, therefore, leaves everything to the imagination except the fact of its own existence, and this it maintains in poetry, for example.

The creation of myth frees the imagination from all concern about consequences, which renders the mind consequent and lets us cope with needless concern, worry, hysteria and the like. Myth-creation, viewed from this angle, is principally curative. While our mind is perfectly sound we have no use for myth. A shock from without causes mental disorder. Given that we care about the state of our mind, we will avail ourselves of myth, so as to recreate order. The recreation aspect of it is important, but also the fact that, all going well, we do not return to the previous order but we turn to a new one, which can be compared to the previous one in terms of growth, by which I mean spiritual growth, implying improved capacities for love, understanding, enjoyment and suchlike.

It's a stupid sort of activity to bother ourselves about whether something is 'really a myth' or 'really a poem'. We all exist in fact, whether we know it or not and whether we admit it or not, and it is a ridiculous suggestion that we need some ideal smart-person to show us how to exist so that subsequently we can recognize the facts – or conversely, to tailor-make facts for us beforehand in response to which we can then go ahead and exist. We exist in fact from the moment we first glimpse the light of day, so that our factual existence ought to be taken for granted. This ought to be done, and the failure to do it makes us guilty. We heap punishment on our heads, in other words, until we agree to accept what is freely given here and what cannot be earned or achieved. (I am conscious of the fact that I have moved into the realm of myth now, by the way.) As soon as we accept, the constraint of the imperative of course disappears and we can then go ahead and discriminate liberally and choose freely, according to our own faculties and persuasions.

A chronic unwillingness to accept and cherish the gift of our factual existence as human beings, and an abuse of myth, an insistence on the fabrication and manufacture of myths, a clamour for false-coinage, go hand in hand. One may pit oneself against this perversion prophetically in the hope of some salutary intervention, but this involves risks and provokes danger, since one is liable to be misled by the weaknesses one adopts for the sake of affecting a therapy. One is reminded of the treatment for addictions, and the required period of drying out, the interval of time in the dessert. Mystics document it as a stage in spiritual advancement.

Given my factual existence and my acceptance of it as such – and also given that I need no evidence to know or believe that I am but my being includes such evidence, for others primarily and only secondarily for myself – I create myth already simply by being more intensely, being not <u>what</u> I am, since I am not a thing, but <u>who</u> I am, because I am, after all, a person.

So we are, and that is existence; and then we are more intensely, more powerfully, and we are persons, and that is myth. I cannot put it more simply or more clearly. We might even add that the intensification of our being, in our case here, is poetic.

Not all poetry perseveres to the extent of myth, and if it does not, we can hardly say that it falls short of it, because the end of poetry is not myth, and myth is not its purpose, but the eternity of the inner man. But some poetry (or painting, etc.), in particular transcendental poetry, points to the very personality of the universe, which happens also to be – naturally and of course, whichever way you look at it – the universality of the person. Transcendental poetry advances the universality of a person, of the particular person involved with the poetry, reading or writing it, while myth celebrates the universality of the person. That shouldn't be so difficult to understand.

That myth is a celebration, insofar as we do not separate it from, but compare it to, poetry, shouldn't come as a surprise. It is, after all, an arrival. Our old friend the plant comes in handy here as a metaphor. It flowers into poetry and fruits into myth. Lets make the metaphor work for us and not get lost in it. We will not try to see it from the plant's point of view. Endowing a plant with a personality may be fun but it won't help us here. So fully conscious of how we accept and take for granted our factual existence, being sound in mind and limb, we value the flower and we esteem the fruit, and we gratefully take the plant for granted. Sure it all makes perfect good sense. We esteem a ripe apple all the more for the fact that it disintegrates in time, because this means that on one hand we will be able to eat and digest it rather than setting it on a mental shelf, and on the other hand it means the propagation of new life, in this case of the species.

Myth is a celebration by us human beings of the fact that we have arrived. Nutrition and propagation are implied here too, though entirely from within, because now we are the plant, and no human being can step outside of humanity (enough said, really) and use the human being as a metaphor, to help him explain – what? God? Nonsense!

Myth, then, as this celebration, takes time too but in comparison to poetry it takes eternal time, which is not a very, very long time, but time itself, not metaphorically perceived as a straight line.

And since it takes time, albeit time itself, eternal time, myth nourishes and propagates: it nourishes human being and propagates humanity. It nourishes your human being and my human being – we are both human beings, are we not? – and it propagates our humanity, which means generally that humanity will exist where previously none existed, and you can apply that to parts and aspects of yourself, or to the human race as such (raising of the dead) or to mankind (salvation) or you can – but here my joy runs over and I have to remember who I am talking to, no offence. The universal nativity is a pleasure too precious not to be shared, so if we ever meet face to face, and whenever we meet face to face, we will share it. However meanwhile the dead letter has to intervene.

When we talk about myth in comparison to poetry (or music, etc.) we might call this too mythology, and this does not imply that myth is devoid of poetry, but rather that poetry is not necessarily myth. In comparison we do not destroy the nature of each and we preserve their character and attributes. Begin, however, to talk about myths and you have nothing in your hand but the peel of the apple. Talk about mythologies and you have but the seedless core. I take great care in deciding what is worth saying because I know all too well, from experience in the flesh, how every bit of nonsense I talk eventually creeps up from behind and bites me.

Now although it makes no sense to talk or write in terms of myths or mythologies, as though such things existed rather than being falsehoods and lies, which decidedly do not exist, this does not take away from the manifold variety of myth, from the great and all-embracing diversity of it, and from the fact that we may come across it where we least expect it. And if a tale is mythic, it is still a tale and not a myth, and if a story moves into the realm of myth it is still a story.

Those who feel that they owe it to themselves to quarrel with this, ought to remind themselves that the best we have is eternal life and its happiness and that it borders on the internal, with all its ups and downs, into which we may accidentally stray from time to time, but let us not confuse it with our natural abode and let us not try to define existence and reality from within delusion, in terms of delusion, but let us get back out as quickly as possible into the light, the sunlight and fresh air, and maybe next time, when 'evil comes into the world' we will not have to let it use us but we will know how to deal with it, on our own terms, mythically.

Ah well, that is one way of putting it. I suddenly find myself wearing rather thin at the edges. The written word is the myth, the mythic entity, presently at my disposal so I intend to make use of it to deal with this problem. There. I feel better already.

The myth? Always in praxis. The letter as figure or graph. Myth-making of the sort that holds water. Language itself as myth. Transcendental talk leading to speech. But make no speeches. Mythology – literature – rhetoric.

And we should not act as though there had never been a human being who had taken it upon himself to dedicate his entire life on earth in such a way that it would guarantee his return after death as living myth, or better, live myth, which in turn, among other things, allows us to speak of poetry and myth as we did. 'Original myth' made it possible for you and me to create myth, but we do not compare ours to his except in shape, and shape is given fresh every time, not copied or based on a model, though we may build a model in order to aid us in our understanding, as we have done elsewhere.

Creation itself is the shape of all life, of the life we live, and of the life to come, which we live in abundance. The world in which we live is open now to the world to come, in which we live in abundance.

> The fool has said in his heart:
> There is no god – and his lips
> utter falsehoods, straight or crooked.
> The clown says with his lips:
> There is no god – not so in his heart,
> where falsehood lies underfoot.

> In whose heart does god speak,
> commanding the lips to do likewise
> and yet they obey eagerly?
> On whose lips does truth blossom
> nourished by the loving senses,
> willing to bear fruit in the heart?

Wisdom ideal, knowledge empirical,
let no man make strife there.
Oh, for the understanding, ah, for the pleasure,
let no man seek disparity here.
Western personality, eastern communality,
let no man find separation there.

*

Even the transcendence of the flesh
makes no difference if the wine
flows like excrement in the gutter.

Even the passionate survival of truth
may not alter the walls of the castle
or penetrate to the garden of the rose.

The power enhanced by the tame horse
perishes before the onslaught of love
and our vision must fend for itself.

*

That old greybeard seated on clouds has
        had to make room.
Hordes of demented immigrants march
        across his tomb.
We who live by the words entrusted
        into our hands
listen to voices that make no promises,
        no familiar demands.

Old dances, folk tunes practiced by
        children on fire,
cherished from time immemorial, add to
        the heart's empire
and the sky, aglow from early heat,
        musters its forces

of women in armour, men on wheels,
    children on horses.

This will cause us agony, hours of
    dreamless watching,
stooped in front of our tyrants, and our
    plight is catching.
Nowhere shall the game of love be
    painless, invented.
Many shall lose their way now in a
    sky that is rented.

*

Oh sadness crowning our wits' end,
boredom singular, bombarding
what is left once the mind has
vacated the premises, the body its roost –

nothing to crow about now, dear me,
only this corner to sit in,
vainglory patching the firmament,
and the brown women with slanted eyes
enchanting their flesh to music.

Tribal confessions in newspapers
still make the blood whirl.
The telephone rings, you leap to your feet –
but this too ends in desolation.

What follows, kings have wept over,
stewards of riches beyond fantasy have
engraved on tablets, and the
children of beggars have greedily devoured,
remaining circumspect.

*

I am not music, not grail, healing
the women left with men to bear.
I scour hearts for spiritual blood.
The last age recognized itself in my
peril there, stretched against the white
wall, and I have thought this over.

I watch over the children, let them
play games in down-pouring contentment.
I amaze at night with sweet love –
its memory next day nags the brain,
giving to dreams reality's savour.
My hand forces life from stones.

*

Transcendental poetry renders the truth palatable.

At the point where poetry becomes myth, or where myth is generated from poetry, there is a crisis, and it is of the nature of a breakthrough. In transcendental poetry, limits are set for the senses but in such a way that they encompass the possible. The critical point is reached when enough such limits have been achieved so that the senses are whole and not for the time being in need of temporal measurement. We have a free choice then, the freest choice ever, either to relish and cherish this fullest possible achievement of our senses, in happiness and satisfaction, or else to abate this life in the interest of others so that they may take advantage of it and have the use of it for themselves.

The creation of myth, however, does not impoverish the creator, any more than the choice not to create myth but simply to create diminishes the creator. He is only diminished or impoverished if he chooses less than freely, as though under some constraint, either physical or mental. However in that case he neither creates nor does he create myth but at best he shows evidence of the crisis and becomes critical himself.

54

Mythology, the science of myth, which is knowledge for the sake of understanding myth, clears the way for us in the interest of eventual myth creation and establishes a link between myth and the perceptive human heart.

Religion can therefore be seen in this light as practical mythology, when we take advantage of the knowledge mythologically gained and put it to good use. The accent is on the use being good, rather than smart or specific, etc. Good use involves all manner of things and allies them to human conduct. The acceptability of human conduct, then, in the light of myth, is what makes for the religious life, centred in a human god and lived in the company of divine human beings.

This has brought us around to what I would like to call religious, or good poetry. It depends on truth insofar as it relies on myth, which persuades us to call it good, and it interprets myth and brings it into common usage, for which reason we call it religious. Remember that the nature of goodness implies an interest in the selfless domain, while religion demands that this domain become personal, singular and specific:

> With open eyes do not stare into space
> but recognize the good will of the nation.
> From beneath, experience the earth's heat,
> transmit this to the next person you meet.
>
> Do I remind you of the season's change
> while yet these spirits arrange and rearrange
> everything your heart has acquired, your mind
> grasped, everything you had ever expected?
>
> But the fine bones of this turmoil and maze
> from the beginning could not have been broken,
> nor shall the ox that stands on ceremony yield
> one inch of its electro-magnetic field.

Scoff if you must, but then turn
and watch the towers of Megalopolis burn
with a cold eye, detached and divorced,
separate from the aesthetics of carnal destruction.

*

When we say that good poetry interprets myth we mean that it lays bare the mystic character of it and makes it available to the inner senses.

The mystic character of myth guarantees its invulnerability to criticism and allows it to operate, by the same token, as a face to the will and as a countenance to the intellect.

Invulnerability to criticism is important because, as we pointed out elsewhere, where there is criticism there cannot be any critique, but critique is precisely what we need if we intend that the character of myth should become more effective. The artificial or accidental gap between perceiving subject and effective object closes, eventually and voluntarily, due to the poetically administered critique, and then I become mythical, which means that I am real.

Criticism, on the other hand, aggravates and increases the separateness of object from subject, hoping thereby, I suppose, to play down the difference of the two, and so naturally soon enough neither exists.

But objects and subjects exist, and will always exist, so that they may come together in the interest of living and to the attainment of more life. Consequently, at this stage of the game, we can say plainly that the choice between criticism and critique is critical, perhaps even absolutely critical.

Invulnerability to criticism is important on another count, in that the mind is left free, either in terms of will or intellect, to give itself over entirely to considerations of shape, rather than having to concentrate on approximations of form and content, or to discipline itself towards considerations of burden and carrier, or even to exhaust itself due to calculation of cause and effect. The mind can organize itself with respect to shape, and eventually it becomes shapely.

Mystical experience could be described as transformation of outward to inward experience, and when we speak of the inner senses we do not by any means wish to exclude the awareness of what goes on around us, but it is a particular awareness of it that is determined by us, with a view to observing truthful connections and true determinants or points of reference. But mystical experience is open at both ends, so to speak; it cannot begin well unless it ends well – which reveals its relation in time. Or, to put it more concretely, mystical observation cannot help but end in mystical service, which brings us to the aspect of the poetry we called religious. No independent or external moral intention lies at the bottom of this service and no derived conviction from dogma motivates it, but the observation and the service are one. If we see it as service we know that we do it to benefit others, without excluding ourselves of course, and this not in response to a request or hopeful of gratitude. What we make available we naturally make use of ourselves right away, and it stands for others to make use of as they see fit. If we see it as observation we recognize how we return to things and to beings what is in fact theirs to begin with, without concerning ourselves over questions of sin and guilt and punishment, so that restitution becomes an automatic technique of our activity.

> I see death question woman and man,
> stepping up close at night while sleep
> stands off, turning its face to the wall,
> and death shakes the foundation.
> The man-in-the-street's nervous condition
> alerts him, he feels with each step
> how the pavement approaches and recedes,
> and houses pass him on both sides.
> The man-behind-the-counter's digestion
> has failed him and he must attend
> to his intake of cholesterol, as he puts it,
> because fat has conditioned his heart.

The lady-from-the-housing-estate's image
as the gritty purveyor of sensible good cheer
has given way under the weight of survival
and now she uses a walking aid.
Death questions me during the night
and I sit up gratefully, to create an answer
and he turns and walks away unaided,
both of us richer for the experience.

*

The character of myth is mystic, implying observation and service as one.

The personality, on the other hand, of myth is mysterious. This means that myth becomes personal in a mysterious way and that a person is mysterious to the extent that his make-up is mythic.

Here we have to get used to thinking of personality not so much as the behaviour of a person but as the possession of a face or the attribute of countenance.

To have a face, strictly speaking, means to be self-conscious without being self-conscientious, to be aware without being doctrinaire, to be able to reflect on oneself via the agency of one's environment. I am not always a person. I do not always and everywhere automatically possess a face. When and wherever I do, my environment is clear and distinct.

But this clarity and distinction of my environment is its mature fruitfulness, in short its wealth. In fact we can say that in its wealth our environment is nothing else. It is our wealth. In this nothing mysterious remains; all is revealed and clear. We see as we are seen, we hear as we are heard, we touch as we are touched. But the mystery exists where this wealth does not, in short wherever our environment is not distinct and clear but to some degree involved with us and we in it. The greater the involvement, the deeper the mystery; and the greatest involvement, or least distinction, causes mystery itself to hide itself away and we move blindly and grope stupidly, vexed by boredom, beset by tedium, forced to stare everywhere at the all too familiar 'face' of our self staring back at us and refusing to be something else.

But it is still our environment, whether wealth or self, and so we always have the power to make of it what we would and we shouldn't wait for money or friends in high places before we get started, because then we will never start. Better to give our money away and turn away from our high friends and then we have already started. But this is old hat.

Wealth as the countenance of our surroundings surely is not so difficult to grasp. Then mystery as the background and predisposition to that wealth should easily reveal itself.

Now if instead of environment we say myth, and instead of countenance or face we say personality, it should come to our understanding more readily how the personality of myth is mysterious.

> A wholly new reality
> rides in on dappled steed.
> You too have known these things I own,
> the trestle that supports the rose,
> the leaning reed.

> You too have slept in snow and kept
> the dream hidden
> far from the clamour of the bell,
> cracked bronze, ribbed steel
> cursing the joy you feel.

> You have silenced more than once
> the inner voice's inner sound
> and then not found,
> like thistledown, anxiety's spell
> manageable in mind.

Therefore ride now
on dappled steed through swaying reed
as though the noise meant what it means
or bully your way forward
up to the cliff's edge.

*

All has gone empty.
No more the shell of the cosmos proves
a house near the sea distinguishable from the sea.
No moon or stars lighten the nocturnal burden,
we sit desolate in crowds on flat rock
and after a thousand hours there is
still no tomorrow.

Where has the sheer joy in our liberty gone,
the delight in flying, soaring beyond hope,
beyond those pyramids, whose giddy heights
point straight into an endlessness of space,
but nothing fathoms the flesh there,
one cannot fall in love.

Can any man mouth
the catechism of creation with impunity?
Some would say that such a
simple thing as a cloud
must be accounted for.
I remember looking at you, and you said:

I lack certainty concerning the testimony of my eye.
When you touch me that is no guarantee
of a response within me of any sort.
It seems I have very little ability
to regulate the conditions on which I exist,
under what circumstances I feel love or loathing –
or anything for that matter.

We have what it takes to feel as we wish:
I wanted to say, but
no sound escaped my lips.
Besides, although I
knew that death had been mastered
and understood how it had been done,
being able to see through all these things
since childhood,
there was nothing I could do
to master your death for you,
this being reserved for you alone,
your opportunity to create
yourself and your environment.

And still I feel,
when dimly I perceive
from the past an ill wind blowing:
you could have done more.

*

Renewal of Society from Within:

What a lovely sounding phrase!
I wonder what it means.
Would you mind, Mr. Babbington,
if I shake and rattle it a bit?

I wonder who is this Mr. Babbington.
He reminds me of someone I saw once
standing with his back to a white wall
and all the members of his small clique
bowed and scraped to him like turkeys,
clucked and veiled eyes for him like owls.
How so much more expressive than their
bird counterparts, I thought, and I
joined them, oozing false affection.

That way, in case it should occur to you
to ask why I did such a thing, I learned
some of the universal laws of Society,
for these pertain equally to all things,
human or otherwise, alive or dead,
as we say when we fear contradiction.

For there, in front of me on the grass, lay
a dead snake, belly up, beautiful to behold.
Go back now and read once more from the beginning.

There are those who would taste Society from within
and I say to them: Go, by all means, go!
Refresh your memory among stone, crystal and sphere.
Hew down the ash, and fear not –
I was going to say: the destruction of the nest
but that might be going too far.
I could not begin to be particular:
pipit, thrush, the peculiar wren –

but nevertheless I say: Wallow in it.
Check in books how you may scientifically overcome
the glaring discrepancies built into all
merely cerebral calculations, while
such a thing as Society
flaps its wings according to the same rules
and I shall not tire of the comparison.

Good Lady, there is Lord Babbington,
he has been Sired and Knighted.
I find his stance with back against the wall
both interesting and refreshing to contemplate.

In his hand he holds a stone,
weighing it, to test its weight,
and how the earth finds this stone
socially attractive escapeth not his

illimitable gaze, his use of
fine eyes, technologically boosted:
horn rimmed spectacles, I mean.

But he glances in my direction
and spits. Have I deserved such treatment,
oh friends of the Society of the Wreath?
Come, stand by me.
Let us link arms, in exclusive embrace,
of inner, private space,
where the eagles shall not detect
the rotting flesh.

Peck peck –
peck peck peck – pause – peck.

There you have it.

Never speak to me of the Society of Saints,
of a wholly-holy alliance of the few,
an Elite, mystification for its own sake
or the speedier attainment of communal ends,
it makes no difference, they are all sheep
that are running away from the shearing.

Would you not spend the rest of your
linkage to the food chain barking back at
the guard dogs of Society, then must you

fear not the odd grammatical contortion,
seated on a bale of hay behind the barn,
trousers ripped by twisted ends of wire,

and Lord Babbington floated down from the
Dovecot, breathing in circles of flesh as he
spiralled, fully aware of his grandeur.

Sat beside me on bale,
hinted at God's Glory,
for the conservation of which he had the
golden key tucked under his left wing,
and spoke to me reassuringly,
thus:

Good friend, dear friend,
companion on many an adventure
through circles of fire,
please let me enhance my body warmth
here beside you on this bale.
Ignore these feathers.
Think of me as an eminent
petitioner for world peace.
I have come from afar:
look, my dovecot in the sky,
whence pointed your pyramids
several ages (verses) ago.
You must remember.
Snuggle up close, please,
my blood runs thin, so thin.

Would you not consider an
Alliance of Free Spirits, feathered
like myself, or not, as you please,
with might and right and fit for fight?

(Oh Babbington, old rabbit ears, I thought,
though somewhat shaken in my composure
by the mere worldly presence of his
other-worldly magnificence.)

This was my reply:

Oh precious origin of sound,
was hast du mir ins Ohr geraunt![1]
what have you whispered in mine ear,
mir scheints du ziehst mich fort von hier.[2]

You draw me onward and beyond
wo sonst kein himmlisch Wesen wohnt,[3]
where nothing lives, no heavenly thing,
kein menschlich Zeug noch Erdending.[4]

Babbington looked flustered
but mustered his courage,
suppressed his outrage,
hid in mellifluous tones,
excused himself from any
further to-do with
such a box of tricks because,
quote: he lacked the key, unquote.

Every question of morals has
two sides, he insisted, and
you have given me only one.

You only see one, I offered,
hesitantly, to be sure, aware
of his superior sense of occasion.

And besides, if you chose to see both,
it would still only be one to you,
because of your overweening suspicion.

An aspect of his face signalled contrition.
A sidelong glance with an eye that glittered,

---

[1] what have you whispered in my ear?
[2] it seems you draw me away from here.
[3] where no other heavenly being lives,
[4] no human stuff nor earthly thing.

the skinny, horny beak, agape slightly,
so that I saw the arrow-headed tongue,
and then the cocky tilt of the head
to take me in with the other eye instead:
I have seldom experienced such fascination.
The enchantment of the expanding ruff,
the scissor shape of wing against wing,
above the ample thigh the downy fluff –

I nearly chuckled – but I'd had enough.
Being sane and sound in mind and limb
I would not provoke the mystery of the kill.
Reason, sweet reason, in my right hand,
in my left the thrust of sexual stuff,
(forgive me, Babbington, if my taste offends,
we must bring this matter to a close,)
I gored the fellow neatly from beneath.

Just one time he cried out, in bloody spasm: Ah
your metaphysical God, do not betray his trust!

Oh I trussed him, I trussed him, to be sure.

I plucked and trussed and roasted him and then
I ate his flesh, his bowels and bones and all.

Good grief! Was that absolutely necessary?

Oh yes.
Let me confess.
I drank his blood too,
gathered the feathers in a bag
to stuff my quilt and pillow later.

This eagle was no second-rater.
The sinews provided me with gumption,
the eyeballs with a look of love,
the others with the making thereof.

The beak, finest of its sort,
would lend me stamina in sport.
The skull I wear suspended from a chain
around my neck. It brings on rain
when I rub it during a drought,

or, when too much water floods the plane,
another rub brings the sun out again.

Truth caters to the moods of man.
Never sacrifice your burden to the powers.
The social sphere would thwart us here
or float off with our better nature
into realms for which neither poor nor rich,
nor man nor god have nomenclature.
So renew Society from within by all means:
the effective broom its own house cleans.

*

Metaphysical poetry – that must indeed be the name for it. It pretends that a supernatural world exists, attracts our attention to it, and then transforms, transmits – transubstantiates – until the spiritual world, which is to say: reality, takes its place.

The entire so-called realm of the metaphysical exists only in poetry therefore, in music and painting, and its reason for existing there is plainly in the service of the physical. By the same token, I suppose, should the realm of the supernatural serve the natural.

However unless we distinguish between the metaphysical and the supernatural we cannot get to the crux of the matter.

It might be wise if we remind ourselves here how one law in fact rules and regulates everything. Against this is set the erroneous and widespread belief that everything is divided in two. (I use the term 'everything' in all thoughtfulness.) But this division in two, allegedly by laws, is discovered to go on 'ad finitum' once one gives it credence, and so, eventually, it would have to decimate itself, as it in fact does here and there. In order to slow this regress down, idols are set up, and their task is to persuade that two laws can exist side by side, not extinguishing one another, but in some constant strife, tension, etc. These idols are sanctioned, ritualized, and to go against them means an opening up to the general view of the underlying impossibility of their existence in reality.

So we must set aside for a moment this widespread and popular assumption that reality is divided and we can keep in mind all the vast systems of activity and industry which testify to the misguided effort to maintain what is basically falsehood. In the absence of such sustained effort the system would collapse under its own weight.

Now there is in the world also a sizable presence of recognition of this effort, and out of this recognition flows the whole body of orthodox dogma and doctrine, wherever it does, and it makes it its task to set up trinities by which this above mentioned division may be unified and healed. The process of reunification is undertaken by positing two functional, apparent opposites, whose function it is to attract and trap, as it were, the two opposed factions for their own good, usually by letting them believe they can pursue their mutual destruction-construction, their 'sustained contradiction', even better under the auspices of the orthodox agency, and then bringing the truth to bear on them. For the sake of unity the apparent duality of art is opposed to the false duality of the idol.

Before the fox lets us get even close enough so that we can free it from the snare, a delicate operation, we may have to administer some tranquillizing influence, because for a while the fox may fear we wish to do it harm.

The realm of the metaphysical then can be viewed as a kind of battlefield where the good guys pretend to be and are seen to be bad in order to convert the bad guys, who in their turn interpret the realm of the metaphysical as a final resting place or, which amounts to the same, as nothing at all. That may be the most risky way to put it but it points nonetheless in the right direction, as a parable. Metaphysics as something in itself has nothing going for it at all. I can indulge myself in metaphysics at the expense of mature human freedom, for example, and a more honest description of me then would be that I try to live a lie. Or I can use metaphysics as an instrument to get the best out of myself, and when I've got it, I lay the instrument down.

So the realm of metaphysics must be mastered if it is not to overwhelm us. To the extent that it overwhelms us we turn, picturesquely speaking, into the living dead who steadfastly believe that the dead are still alive somewhere.

Now let's compare this to the realm of the supernatural. Here it comes as a shock to some people if they are told that they can be born again and that they will never die, or, if they die, they will live again. What could this mean? How do they stand in relation to those who deal in or with metaphysics?

The spiritual organic being, or the real person, if you like, makes the relationship possible, hypothetically, theoretically or in fact.

Metaphysics is hypothetical: theory is supernatural, it comes down to that, and all questions of use or abuse, of propriety or misapplication, of bigotry or common sense, must be answered afterwards.

Supernatural entities are projected quite naturally by the live imagination, and this does not argue against their reality. What does argue against it is the disposition with which we approach these entities, the attitudes we assume when we advance towards them, the moods we harbour, the sentiments we foster, the affects we produce, as we propose to enter into a relationship with them – this argues against their reality, as we test our own against theirs for the sake of improving on what we have already and adding on to it; or else it militates against our own reality and little by little removes it, destroys it, falsifies it; one or the other, depending on our approach. Disposition, attitudes; moods, sentiments and affects; all these either work for us or against us as we approach the supernatural entities no one can coldly avoid, depending whether we see them as linked organically to ourselves and consequently under our personal jurisdiction, or whether we consider ourselves as under their influence and at their beck and call. In the first instance our 'organism' will become spiritual; in the second one we really have no 'organism' to speak of and only fool ourselves from time to time by manufacturing a false image of organic being and 'existing' at its mercy for as long as it allows us to get away with it.

Supernatural entities abound and they always will do. There is no need to mention names and provoke sectarian strife. A poet wants to live somewhere so that he can work effectively, and he chooses to live at the time that he happens to live, because no other time would suit his purpose as well. Also, his own natural instinct is to become familiar with these supernatural entities, so that he can develop against them and grows on them. In that sense metaphysical poetry could as readily and and suitably be called supernatural poetry, because the hypothetical preparation amounts to the same as the supernatural practice, and the metaphysical application amounts to the same as the theoretical use:

*

At the five-fingered bridge,
as we called it as children
because of the way it
reaches into the valley,
a spirit has these many years
kept its residence.

I would rather not say
how often I have knocked on that door
and a voice from within spoke,
saying:

What have you done?
How have you betrayed my trust?
When will the time be full?
What have you done to
advance the fullness of time?

The ambiguity of all these questions
made me hesitate
with a hand on the doorknob
and I did not enter.

Several times,
provoked by an insatiable curiosity,
I racked my brains
and then it was as though a curtain parted
and a light shone through,
though within me,
and the emphatic nod of the head at the window
only put me off,
so I disregarded that exercise
for the time being
and dedicated myself to the
farsighted beacon of that light,
wishing it might be otherwise,
sometimes strangled by the outward necessity,
otherwise content with the norm.

But the spirit
cries out behind the window,
ambitious for remembrance,
jealous, as it seems, of my
liberty as I ranged among the hills
like my friend Wordsworth,
in whose company I then felt safe,
since we both espoused
the beauty of pastoral violence.

Not that I would have called myself
a heathen, even before that, though
the heath attracted me powerfully,
and the many tastes, scents and
flavours springing from its soil

and flourishing there like a
comb in a hive stocked by
invisible bees, drew me down and

away from myself, from you too,
invisible reader, dearest companion
now, that my work has selected me.

Bridge, beneath your arches
my patience grew to proportions
when first I sketched the distant tree line
and cast the stone behind the hare,
and crushed the voice of first desire
while overhead the tramcars rumbled.

Why not still stand there unmaligned,
five-fingered, stretching across what is
known as the valley of desolation
from ancient days, not that I would
follow in sages' footsteps there,
because my idle thoughts are spoken for,
also the memory blowing in my temples
of heroes tragically tied to wheels

draws on and on these
flowery seashells in its wake.

*

Or was it a ghost?
No spirit at all, but a ghost,
beckoning behind the window pane?
And the bridge was my own invention?

Courage, my friend, you will find
much to replace this ghost, though
not outside there,
nor inside here
but be not afraid.

Should I not protest that I was taken in?

But you were not taken in,
neither did you enter,
you have said so yourself.

But all those sweet and doleful memories – !

Never let that cause you
one moment's hesitation now.
Where the grain parts, the scythe mows
and the field spreads to beyond the horizon.

Then I am not concerned for my life.
No more can the mosquito make me tremble
nor the dragon's laugh; the illusions have
done their trick : god bless the illusions.

We have given up child ways.
Shall we curse the dolls now
and step on the rattles
and fling soft toys out the window
under a motor car?

Not so!
Speak softly, and make amends,
and patrol the border surrounding the
playing field. Eat with both eyes open.

And what of those who still insist
that the ghost is spirit
and that the bridge links
failures to successes,
betterment to information?
Shall we season them with the
onslaught of our word?
Do we care to do this –
or do we care more not to do it?

I am explicable to the end.
I can make no promises because
there are no more promises, only
the settlement of the sphere,
the establishment of the vineyard.
Let politics become politics
and carry the burden of restitution
where the spoon and the bowl stand idle.

I have become
wanton in my misery.

By my love shall you know me.

*

When we recognize truth for what it is, namely ourselves in recognition; when we see truth for what it is, ourselves in sight, and we
speak truth as ourselves in speech: not relations, equations and approximations – then we can bring ourselves eventually to say exactly what we
mean to say, we can see what we want to see and understand perfectly.

Poetry now becomes the experience of ourselves in truth. We make
no distinction between poetry and prose except by the merest appearances, between poetry and painting except by the finest of illusions,
between poetry and music except by the most cursory of disguises.

The hope we hold out for the expression of ourselves recoils
creatively, reacts in discipline, responds responsibly: in short, we
have no more desires to desire, no feelings to feel, no thoughts to
think, but we desire, feel, think, period. Or, if we like, we exist in
terms of poetry, of poetry and the truth, for example:

In dream the rain pours down on earth,
engendered by the experienced moon.
The search for love is search for death
and we admire how high we fly

and quicken then the downward pace –
all tricks to make an angel swoon.

Would it not impress a god more
if we found his being linked with our own?
The will was razed ready to the ground,
the bell secured by wit and rope,
by far too promising in scope.
Wild men will always cling to hope.

*

True poetry loses nothing in translation, as we have ascertained
elsewhere; in fact it improves in it:

Wo sich des Menschen Grösse zeigt,
dort überspringt er gern sein Wesen.
Aus Blütenkelch und reifer Frucht
liest gern Erzogener Pflanzenzucht,
unmöglich dem, der Schein verflucht
und Schatten sucht im Sinn des Bösen.

Gleich im geliebten Reich der Kunst
übertriffst du selten jedes Ganze
und drohst nur dir, verwunschenes Tier,
und leugnest, ach, du kannst dafür,
denn Alles übertrifft Dich hier,
du Sonnensohn, aus Stein und Pflanze.

*

So wherever, in poetry, we concern ourselves foremost with
truth, rather than with experience, say, or the world, or justice, or
feeling, etc. we arrive also at the purely organic limitations of language. To translate poetry, for instance, is not the same as to translate
words, meaning, sense, because when we translate poetry from one
language into another we move not one, but all of these and more,
and the translation of true poetry into another language illustrates
how that other language is susceptible in the same way, organically.

75

A language suits us to the extent that we make use of it organically. This implies that while we use it, we remain aware of the fact that we are using a language, and that it is not abusing us, which can also happen, and it does to the extent that we are not aware. Even if English were the only language left on earth it would still be profitable, perhaps all the more so, to keep in mind that we use a language.

The fully organic use of a language is attained in true poetry. Here we are finally able to let a language take care of itself, as it were, but only because of who we are and what we are while we write or read such poetry. (In painting we use colour and in true painting we use colour organically.)

But just as we ought to take our own factual existence for granted, so we should assume as guaranteed the organic suitability of our language. We should do that, just as we ought to do the other, and this comes as a constraint, as I pointed out earlier, but as soon as we take the one for granted and assume the other as guaranteed, the constraint is lifted and truth can work for us from within.

A terrible mistake is made wherever that constraint is analyzed or studied. It is part of our birthright and must be acted upon, not separated out and away so that we can get rid of it.

Translating this organic imperative into a moral imperative has worked in a way for a while in the past, but the only way it can after all be said to have worked is in that it, the moral imperative, stood in the way, here and there, of a downright organic perversion, and it helped to slow down the degeneration of the human race wherever it threatened to take that course, even as that world did which it helped to prop up. So while we have no quarrel with that world, we nevertheless realize all the while that we can do better than that and learn how freely to get along without it.

While there was such a thing, I suppose, as the moral imperative, as part of a systematic thought process, we cannot technically speak of 'the organic imperative', precisely because such a thing as <u>the</u> moral imperative would again have to pertain to a system, but <u>an</u> organic imperative does not. It simply presents us now and again with a need, a choice and a challenge, particularly within the framework of our carnal experience, and peculiarly linked to our persuasions, convictions and opinions with respect to our native rights as – an individual among many.

This business of 'one among many' hits home right away of course, because our pride is linked to it, racial, tribal or individual, and so we can feel it within ourselves, this motion to go against outward constraints, and while virtue is not available to us here, as it would be in the case of a moral constraint, the awareness of this motion cannot escape us, and so we face it and give in to its action upon ourselves.

There, it leaves you alone now,
to face the music, alone now,
nothing else matters much,
be brief, waste no words.

You have nothing else to add,
only the dark gate opens,
you call it the bright gate,
be specific with every breath.

Here once three spirits entered,
you begin with the weak spirit,
you probe the heart's depth
and next your will flourishes.

They have maligned my power,
therefore exercise tyranny here
and favour none, plead with none,
make an end of all things.

*

77

Alone among enemies you wait,
never lee capable of love than now,
your recklessness tosses you and your
fists hold down the table.

Make no one accountable for this
and leave no stone unturned,
be at once everything and nothing
and locate the fellowship of humanity.

Be as quiet as a church mouse
but make a warm place for yourself
where people have nothing to fear from you
and the testimony of youth has ceased.

Then it likens daylight to night,
takes hold of the false animal,
disrobes in front of an unsound crowd,
regularly mistakes your self for its energy.

*

Organically imperative is everything that draws us down and away from the preoccupations of our ego. Voluntarily to leave the ego behind means to transform this imperative into a well of being. From within such a well of being we do what we would:

The greatness of the life we lead
does not depend on that we bleed.
It follows from the life we give
while others bleed and others live.

The blend of what we feel and breathe
and render forth from pleasure's dream
has driven forth and caused to green
these tender shoots and daring buds,

though May still waits for March to pass
and April seems an age away
called 'cruellest month', and flocks of crows
sweep greying clouds from bush and tree.

It seems my mind has waited just
for such a day as this to bear
in forecast womb this present bloom
and every change in hour and room.

Where tired in brook and flooding pond
my image like a silken skein
disconsolate flows, more tired grows
and nowhere men its white face shows,

there city builds, in final rest,
its earth-wide silence-bound domain
and prosperous men who own this land
require no pattern for their dreams.

All darkness leaves a gentle soul
of felt love clinging to the trees
and whispering hushed the thrush imparts
no secrets to profound men's hearts.

For here all water and all air
runs clear as though untouched by pride
and fear has caused no frightful charm
to appear on tongue or cheek or eye

and wasted strength comes doubled twice
returning to the arm and thigh
and tasted fruit gives hunger quick
its appetite and ripens quite.

It ripens where the full heart takes
from curious eyes its tenuous leave

and down from crossbeam and top branch
fine loves and freest affections shakes

and poor moon crowds out hill and dale,
being threatened by an ill-bred storm
so high that starlight cannot cope
but drowns our sight in endless scope.

*

A response to an organic imperative will always at first seem ar-
duous. It seems we would much rather meet like with like, reply to
force with force, but by far the most usual reaction today cuts the sensible person off from his or her organic being and then, since the claim
appears now as a disintegration of the organism as seen separately,
which is to say of the cadaver, continuous measures must be taken to
maintain this cadaver, since unmaintained it would literally fall apart.
Sometimes attempts are then made to reclaim the organism, by way of
all sorts of exercise, but if this is not followed up with some creative
commitment it comes to nothing.

The first step therefore is recognition of the claims our organism
makes on us and a recollection of all the attempts we have made to reject
those claims, usually in the name of some bogus virtue. I find in my own
case that it takes a great deal of peace and quiet even to come to terms
with what I would call my organic human nature. This is probably due to
the cultural bias that today still works against such an interest. We want
to be hard on ourselves and get tough with our body. The pitting against
each other of body and mind has taken on definite, heroic proportions,
the notion of mind over matter, implying self-sacrifice, or sacrifice of
mind to body, of body to mind, is seen by many as a largely laudable affair, when in fact it amounts to no more than a vicious circle and self-
delusion with respect to this fact.

We have to be careful however that we lay no blame,
not on our upbringing, our education, our culture or tradition, not
even on ourselves, because this would go contrary, automatically,
to what we want to achieve in the realm of the organic.

The concept of guilt itself is of course not positive in our present sense, only anti-negative, and the traditional Christian concept of original sin stems, indeed, from the unwillingness to come to terms in a lively manner with our organic being. Original sin is not so bad, however when we compare it to the much more serious subsequent fierce attachment to the systematized prejudice that is meant to slow down and if possible arrest the return to a sound organic relationship. The worse fault is therefore frequently committed by those who condemn the original fault, because condemnation is the very thing that hinders our return to the beginning. In fact there is no way I know of that that would allow us sensibly to apply the term moral to what goes on when we go about reclaiming our original organic nature. Morality is not bad; it contributes nothing to our wholeness. Immorality is bad, but of course we come nowhere near it since we already find ourselves travelling in the opposite direction. Moral poetry is therefore a contradiction in terms, while we could speak of organic poetry which makes it its motive to break out of a moral structure, to contact an organic imperative – and then to liberate the organism as such.

The liberated organism retains all the attributes of law, without, however, contributing to the law as such. And this should ease a great deal of contemporary anxiety. We did say: all the attributes of law, take note, not just some of them. Also, since no contribution to the law is made, we can see how the liberated organism is lawful but not legitimate, and certainly not illegitimate, in the same sense that good spirituality rules out both morality and immorality alike.

Poetry that operates entirely within the confines of the liberated organism has nothing to declare except the fact that it exists:

> Going into these
> strange halls dedicated to
> sincere friendship and the dance,
> reminds the heart of former times

when like today, all neat and tidy,
we allowed ourselves caresses
and pages of books blew
shut; whiling hours away,

finding more to do than kissing
highly unlikely, or meditating
upon that moment where
a life overleaps itself.

Here it leaves less to the
imagination bathed in hues of
sensuous truth than a forced
failure would signify, thankfully,

or imperially the birds cry
havoc and spear-thrusting descend
to break down our defences
and trembling, we give timorously in;

oh, in value of these then
magnanimous moments strung
end to end, fine satisfaction lies,
never lies deeply embedded.

Do cause, as the iris does,
yellow to flirt with the fingertips,
fragile butter skin only to
mirror the foxglove's

fellow entanglement in a love
difficult to embrace, easy to muster,
as hummingbird tonguing,
snowflake visually melting in coolness,

pinecone its fragrance
wafting across in a summer's haze
or to feel in the moist grass
languid the stimulus of lust.

*

And much of the time is spent
fending off ghosts, trivial aspects of
rhyme and reason under duress,
too true to be dreamt away,

bridled tensions shifted
from person to person, and the might
of indifferent genius, flagrantly
lifting its skirts in public,

takes itself far too seriously
to be gently deflected, so
make giant strides quickly or
gather ye poppies under the moon.

*

The liberated organism sustains itself in time and place by virtue of its pure energy, and our task is to utilize that energy. Independent of any utility by us this pure energy runs riot. The idea therefore is to remain watchful and to cultivate patience. The truth of the matter lies in our responsibility and in our accountability. There is a wrong way to go about it and then there is the way to go about it. I would not say that there is a wrong way and a right way, because the choice is not like that. A right way suggests a pick from several and also a standard of judgment, neither of which is the case. When we do have our pick of ways they are all wrong, and the standards are of misjudgement.

I believe that the failure to deal properly with this pure energy when it suddenly arises has caused much of the grief that is commonly put down to an individual lack of capacity and to institutional impotence. Is it not the case that during recent years we have come to think and behave in terms of force and power only where questions of right are concerned, in other words where recognizable standards of judgment operate and can be trusted to persist? And then, naturally, where those standards break down or become suspect, along with the judgment, we become suspicious of force and power, and eventually reject the means along with the end. Whether power is wielded to some bad end or becomes an end in itself amounts to the same in that neither leaves the power open to our proper instruction, and the force is not applied in the only way that exists.

If we feel safe with electro-magnetic forces and nuclear power, this is because we trust the people who manipulate them correctly. If we set those people up on pedestals or forget that they exist and what exactly depends on them, they soon enough make mistakes and we feel the pain, or they abuse their power, and we feel the pain again. But abuse or misuse, in physics, medicine, politics, religion, education the sheer fact of the force and the power remains, forceful and powerful, not yet abused or misused, if you like.

So what I have proposed to show here is how the liberated human organism, as a powerful and forceful entity, is nothing to be afraid of but something to be watched out for; that it should not be killed off at first notice or drugged out of existence right away, but that there are ways and means of dealing with it, even in periphrasis like this, but more especially in terms of poetry, when the word is the inner man.

Now if we mean to discuss this organic power openly we ought to be clear about one thing : There is a poetry which does not allow the human being to admit this power and expends some effort at hiding all evidence of it and at pretending no such thing can exist. Rather than poetry I would call it a poetry, in the vernacular, and descriptively I would call it extinct poetry. As such it enjoys an esoteric, self-congratulatory appreciation by those who belong to the club, and the alignment diverges from academic to pop, the language varies

84

from public to private while the intention alternates between the popular and the commercial. Extinct poetry serves its purpose, but as an anti-negative phenomenon, slowing the regress while values get sorted out. Its affair with truth is peripheral, only where contact cannot be avoided.

But on with the main stream of our activity.

The liberated human organism expresses itself forcefully, we can start with that much. Let us for the time being leave the power of it alone.

The forceful poetic expression of the liberated human organism clears itself a path in terms of a language and so becomes inwardly appreciable. The actual inward appreciation of this force then can simply be called strength, and we know it as integrity, dignity and character:

>Look around you before you judge.

>Let daylight cover your origin before you
>single out any particular
>woman for love,
>man for affection,

>regardless of who you are,
>man in fear of his manhood,
>woman anxious for her womanhood.

>Let children take care of themselves here,
>they share in our predicament
>but choose no alliance with us,
>except perhaps within.

>Look around before you judge.

*

>Of course the sensational drug
>appeals to the young. The old
>prefer their drugs cold.

85

An explosion has ripped
the security from our bowels.
Our harness has slipped.

From within, the sea pounds
the props, tests the hold,
calculates time in breaks,
makes fear give heart away.

I am frightened, like the next man,
of creation exposing my belly,
of emotion racing through my streets,
an inexplicit, reckless yearning,
looting and burning.

A muscle twists, a tendon
flames, a joint silts up.
That windmill on the hill
stands still. Please listen to this.
Make your life less detrimental.

*

Forceful expression was followed by energetic expression, which arises from an application of force to itself, of force to force. Energy is therefore contained. That this can be done is important to remember. If we think that force always has to be expressed, we soon fear it, for we fear it may get out of hand. In this fear the roots of criminality find nourishment. The person is then incarcerated because the human being did not contain the force of the liberated organism. This is unfortunate. Expression is the rudimentary containment of organic force; energy is its radical containment.

The word we use for whatever is both contained and containment is content. The emotional perfection of content is contentment.

Energy as content is given poetic shape simply by its exposure to language. The language supplies the word patterns, both conventional

and grammatical, and so the energy becomes articulate and commu-
nicative:

> Tram cars pelting along at
> a great speed made it
> obvious to me that I must be
> living in a dream somewhere.
>
> You too should ask yourself:
> How often have I trapped my conscience
> along these public highways and
> private byways, and the birds settled
> down around me as though an
> alternate form of existence were
> possible for them?
>
> I prefer to stick to my
> own explanation : Babies take themselves
> too seriously when I'm around; old men
> grunt into themselves, waxy ears
> closing, and the gentle sex – what!
> where? – I'd rather not go into that.
>
> Beauty reforms my heart, but I
> do like idling away the
> dusty hours of a morning,
> living in a dream somewhere.
>
> *
>
> Go to these miserable huts in which
> people live, hiding from the moon
> and they narrow their eyes when you enter,
> you do look brave, you see,
> and no one likes to be seen in your company.
>
> But I do wear this hat to give
> fair warning to all the natives
> and when in the morning I ride out,

prepared for the subtleties of the chase,

amazing things happen to me.
The least you can do is
let me tell you about them.

Ten commandments ride up,
five on each side of me,
armed to their pointed teeth
and the luxury of such company
illustrates the need for taking care.

By my Lord's easy manners,
I detest these ruffians,
they emerge from the underbrush.
I would keep my fingers clean.

Forth from the clouds bursts
miraculous thunderstorm;
I am not educated enough to
interpret these signs sufficiently,
if indeed they are signs,

but I would not quarrel with the postman.

I would rather ride to the next town
and settle down there,
between market place and rose garden,
sell my horse to the highest bidder.

Look, I can see my reflection here,
and yours beside it, does that surprise you?
We make a fine couple, you and I,
ideal and real, Lord John and Lady Jane,
not yet besmirched by the
rabble's lust for sacrifice.

Well, someone
somewhere ought to come out with it,

else everything stays the same through the
centuries, no new tongues wag,
and the explosive nature of nature makes
Sally pull a silly face
when Robert reaches for her hand,
so no wonder comes to pass,
no highland flings are flung
and no sycamores are pollarded.

Make what you will of that,
I can penetrate my own mind safely
some other day, if you think it depends on that.

*

Go out, my light, in here and shine out there
to bring to men this message of glad tiding.

We are alienated from ourselves,
our organs are suffering from starvation,
we belong elsewhere but cannot
bring ourselves to remove ourselves
from this planet quickly enough.

I am angered by the illumination imposed upon
my heart, my brain, my mind, my soul, and

now I am not another person,
now I am the person you love,
the political syndrome of the land
speaks for none other than you
and you should satisfy yourself on this point.

Render unto Caesar what belongs to – no,
do not pronounce the name, make no mention of it,
take your insanity off to another place where
the quick exist and the partially frozen exist
and an impulse sometimes creates much damage.

Or we face the troubles ahead with
renewed vision and a cyclical philosophy.

*

Organic energy invested in language, this energy as the content
of shape and accessible there, due to articulate language: We can
imagine and think physical poetry like that. The physical aspect of
reality is then scientifically included in our deliberations on what poetry is all about, and in addition, of course, we always win more territory for poetic exploration.

Let me out of this sphere!
The world has me trapped
like a chick in its egg
and I would be born.

But no birth is complete without
the simplicity of an experience,
the tree-lined landscape upheld
in the vicinity of an isolation.

Even the miraculous effect of
daylight on my inner self can
totally obscure, properly vindicate
the elusive passions of my flesh.

Consequently I am not of a mind
to prepare myself yet for discovery
beneath the yellow straw, on the
brown field, formally artistic.

*

Energetic language as such is patient of more than just a
nodding acquaintance. The difference between it and literal or
vocal data transfer is immense. Insulation against it commonly takes
the form of nothing less than organic instability and a subsequent
emphasis on such standards as moderation, rationality, harmony,
symmetry and balance, all qualities both excellent and fine in them-

selves, but none of them suitable for the re-establishment of a sound organic constitution, the likes of which is prerequisite if energetic language is to make even a rudimentary impression on ourselves. Given a sound organic constitution, instincts that rest secure in themselves even vis-à-vis all the systematized preoccupations with extinction in our everyday lives, an integrity that allows our person to act without losing itself in the effects of its action, a habit of trust so ingrained that its operations have become reflexive and second-nature; given such a constitution, one thrives on energetic language and seeks it out as with an appetite for food. Standards of comparison are either entirely avoided or taken in stride, but they cannot become means to such ends as pleasantness, likelihood, loveliness, comeliness, smoothness, etc.; nor even their opposites, as happens sometimes in reactions to styles.

Organic instability, however, which we acknowledge usually at first by a revulsion of taste and then by a rebellion of appetite, distaste and disgust, would always be hidden, so that we make a pretence of knowledge and call ourselves experts or we make a show of expertise and call ourselves professionals. The organic instability is then covered over to the extent and degree that our expertise is publicly recognized and our profession is acknowledged. Eventually however these castles in the air must crumble and the organism demands its due.

Its instability is in fact due to a lack of power, and this manifests itself in all our frantic attempts to look and seem as though we were actually powerful when in fact we are not. What has frequently been jeered at as 'the will to power' more often than not by those of us affected even then by the malady, amounts to a will to hide our impotence; but this, as an insight, is nothing either startling or new. Where we need to apply ourselves with fresh vigour is in the action consequent to the insight, where we judge the impotence mercifully and then lay ourselves open to the affect wrought, or rather distraught, by a rather lamentable state of affairs, of emotion, pain and passion all awry, of an interminably ill-considered zeal, zest and enthusiasm, so wondrously wrong-headed and sick at heart at once that it would stand a sane person's hair on end – yet we dare not call it madness, and this because of the organism, not the person, that cries out for the natural vestment of its power. We can actually speak of an organism in such an instance, in the same way that at the start of the modern age one referred to demons that disputed and even re-moved the right of an individual to a personality. Demons could be, and were, cast out. Today such language is obsolete, but:

> By trial and error, hook or crook
>   we wormed our way through.
> The age that spawned rockets into space
> but spurned the sperm cell from the egg,
> fearing nothing like over-population,
>   descent and the lack of descent,
>   has nearly gone unnoticed.
>
> Will our tears blossom as April teases
> from wounds the wonder of a dawning?
> Shared discontent with blood and strife
>   cannot disarm us now.
> We have cast deep down for a progenitor
> whose face bans terror
>
>   and his voice breaks bad bone.

*

> I'm so miserable I could die
> and I want to tell the world about it.
> What does it matter if anyone listens
> or how I feel after I do it?
>
> The worst that can happen to me
> is that you leave me to my own devices.
> I don't mind this lethargy so much
> but I would prefer some spark of life.

*

A terrible feeling, to be worthless,
to suspect that
nobody could possibly want
anything to do with us, because

we can only see the black side of life
while we know there is more to it than that.

I want to participate in
games in the sunshine
and make things happen out there,
but I am afraid of people
and of what they bring out in me.

I have no centre.

Oh, I abound with explanations for it,
all equally curious and worthless.
When the pressure starts to build
I run into a corner of my imagination
and pretend to be on stage.
That way all the lies are justified.

I am vengeful enough to want
someone to jeer at me in this state,
because that will bring their house of cards down
and jumble their jigsaw puzzle existence.

*

Next time I buy myself a house
I'll buy courage along with it
to live in it for a day or two
and the pasture lying around it
is going to have to support me
because I carry my head in a sack.
Too much loneliness buries a man
and he draws out his own entrails.

I don't want to be nagged to death
by people waiting for Martians,
for Supermen, to get them off the hook.

I only want to drink heavy
and lay my roll down in the barn,
so that when the sun rises in the morning

I'll be fresh as a daisy, not half-cocked
and raring to aggravate folks
who never done me no harm nohow.

Lookee there, stranger, (a man with a
cowboy hat, I do believe he
recognized me.) Howdy, stranger!

If that rain keeps up, I'll not
sleep under this tree much longer
because the ground's getting wet.
Hell, we can come an' go as we please,
in this century, the campfires don't
go out any more, and that's a fact.

*

The re-establishment of organic stability necessitates a passage
through the unacceptable. We organize ourselves in line with primi-
tive urges and we make do with whatever comes our way from that
direction, ready to accept the fact that the cause of our inner distor-
tion has been our own neglect of the truth in the past and that consequently it is only natural that we should now wish to reject whatever
tends to remind us of this. And yet there is no way of side-stepping
the issue. In order to have our standards renewed we have to suspend
all standards for a while and operate instinctively, and in this way our
instincts overcome our extinction. It amounts to the same, whether
extinction has set in with respect to taste, intelligence, wisdom,
strength, or whatever, the point being that external reality has taken

on for us to some extent, in fact or in promise, the status of reality as such. We have come to take the shell of the egg for the egg in its entirety. It stands to reason that a period of the 'only natural', as we called it a moment ago, shall have to be gone through in order to reverse the trend, and a great deal of our insistence on force and power in art today stems from the recognition of a bias towards the extinct and from a desire to remedy the situation, or at least to see it altered. Not that force and power are somehow germinally instinctive, but extinction has in fact set in primarily in terms of force and power, and our instincts must choose the same terms if they are to come back into their own rights where they can furnish us in a manner of speaking with the roots of acceptability.

We can only desire, after all, where a stimulus has been created, and if such a stimulus should prove initially unpleasant, desire will need the help of wisdom before it can come into operation, and such a dual sponsorship then will lead us out of our self-imposed incarceration in a detrimental externality, where the 'achievement of life' is 'searched out', basically, as an infinite series of points, as a finite magnitude of feeling, as a performance of the inevitable, as a biased tradition, badly structured, to hold our attention forever, as a dwelling-place beyond the clouds, finally, fantastically pictured, mechanically reached or metaphysically adhered to, at the expense of everything that could even remotely be called the original stuff of the human creature:

> I am a negative individual,
> not suited to the times.
> There stands my house, my car,
> see here my licence to commit adultery.
>
> The way you look at me
> makes me wonder why I live.
> Begging your pardon, Miss,
> I imagined we had an understanding.

*

95

Poetry that springs directly from the human creature like this cannot be said to have anything in common with time or with temporal concerns. It stands ready-made, as it were, prior to our recognition of time, and so it should not be applied in time. The human creature, or the human being insofar as he or she is created, can be turned entirely, by way of the creative process, of operation and organization, into poetry, and understandably this leaves nothing to the comparative intellect. On the other hand we all feel the need from time to time for a thoroughgoing cosmic justification, some indication of our true place right at this moment in the scheme of things. Such attempts fail if we insist on such contribution of our ego as: 'I didn't do it', or 'I did do it but it was someone else's fault', in order to explain our sense of estrangement, bound up possibly with bad conscience phenomena, and the reason they do fail is because they miss the point of cumulative spiritual growth, where the advance may be compared to the past, and very gratefully too, but not in view of some standard outside the two points of reference, because a: obviously such a standard cannot be, and b: the bad conscience resulting from such a false comparison works against the justification we desire in the first instance. Cumulative growth, however, is so thoroughly documented in our time as a false notion of extinct proportions that one might do better to choose another, less inexpedient expression:

> Look around you, but take heart,
> reminisce a while on the past,
> abstain from office where you can;
> the enlightenment of all your faults craves
> an extension out there, where imagination
> has erected signposts which are, you know,
> not automatically to be trusted.

> This is how I speak to myself as March snow
> alternates with spring sunshine and the son
> of man introduces himself to me vicariously.
> You too are permitted to give thought to this,

if the stream of your ideas should ever flow
sluggishly and you sulk by the wayside,
downcast on account of some wrong explanation.

But please, take no notice of me,
nor of yourself for that matter. We relate
so much more elegantly by way of muse,
amusement and leisure, ideas in idleness
conceived, in strength borne, considerably
carried out, leaving the spirit we trust free reign,
either way, and the letter shall not rule us.

Voice spirits bad spirits away before you can
turn the other cheek. Voice leaves the letter
lagging behind, lacking heart for thought,
head for understanding, as though angels,
by some ancient rite, had gained access
to the throne room, and the leopards on the wall
fell in with one another, breathless on occasion.

Timorously you mentioned another time, another
place, too far to reach by telephone or rocket,
and yet it seems, oh my dear seamstress, we can
lay our hand on it, set our mind to it, be
plentifully persuaded, my friend, by a call for
no enthusiastic agitation with respect to it,
by the fullest possible achievement on account.

Why did you not emigrate that time?
Do you remember, we stood on the quay,
some people waved as to parting soldiers,
we wanted to be the first across, yet you
had second thoughts, as happens so often with you,
and now I have to send you pictures here,
snapshots of promises. Never mind, you survive.

I too have been knocked about a bit

by circumstance. I liken myself to those
dwellers on the island called earth whose
ambition it is to flatten the surface of the sphere
and prove no end exists here, but
all ends where neither the myth nor the theme
quite suffices unless we add ourselves in too.

I could coax the rain from the sky if I chose
and opt for the intermediary solution, neither
sin nor saintliness, but moral respect –
or shall we call it the law of the layman,
where I admit my shortcomings openly
and hate cowardice nevertheless, asking
death to remedy the situation in some way.

The point is, none of these work today, not
heaven, not hell, not the world between, and
you can sit there and try to make your
own point until you're blue in the face,
and you get it out, everyone has done you
the courtesy of keeping quiet long enough, but
it did no good because nobody listened.

So please, god, help me stop trying to
make a point. The satisfaction is spurious.
Too much pain gets ignored due to it
and the cold comfort of approving relatives
sits hard with me, because they have no
use for me, nor for the new values I have
sweated out in thoroughgoing isolation.

One must have what it takes today to
know and to ignore according to the spine,
like a boa constrictor, with lidless eyes,
attuned by smell to subtle sex changes,
willing to lie low for weeks on end and

then for a big meal, perhaps not very pretty
but able to survive in the heat of the spirit.

Even the rage situated between my temples
is really your rage, and I hand it over to you
as a gift of flesh under conditions of starvation.
This thick cloud of dust covers you now,
the commercial noises of a popular culture,
so learn to retain a spark of intelligence,
in a squirrel's nest, guarded under your coat.

My most alarming memories scream at me
as though they had just stepped out of a tree,
belabouring the indifferent children of my mind
with a ferocity I would rather not mention in public.
However one must accustom oneself to the times,
look comical if required, prepare for a hanging
with equal ease, or else simulate a happiness.

If nothing else leaves us room for breath,
why not exacerbate our internal organs,
postulate a program of public spending there,
portents of future exhibitions in stone,
the Olympics of the brain, proudly owned up to,
aquatic illuminations, fireworks in the stadium,
probes into the star-studded sky for a dime.

God leaves us no choice today, we have our orders,
we use the same words but speak another language,
so let's not quarrel with the fact that we exist,
let's be good little soldiers and learn our freedom,
please, no more lamenting, no more whining,
leave that to dogs whose masters want to serve them,
no one can tell us any more how to behave.

*

This brings me to the end of a threefold interpretation of the poetic talent. The muse has returned to the home where she reigns supreme. Poetic genius? It helps itself to the fruits of the talent. It transforms itself in terms of talent and takes us along with it, not always the most willing of companions. But in the end we know who knows better. We believe it a bit more successfully every time; and the difference it makes to our lives won't frighten us so much the next time, because each time round the pattern becomes more familiar, the demand for endurance less exacting, the claims on our nerves ... well, one continues.

I have tried, more than anything else, I think, to testify to the protean character of poetry, to its usefulness and serviceability, as a life-giving and life-creative thing, so suitable to an individual human being's search for value and meaning, for an immutable point of reference at a time when so much seems in flux, as a tool for breaking through hardened attitudes and ritual association.

My own experience of poetry is as of a fire – of the fire. It warms, heats, burns – consumes and cleanses. That is also why it offends me deeply to see poems set up on altars and worshipped, poetry treated as though it amounted to anything at all irrespective of the human being intimately concerned about his spiritual growth. And I realize that one cannot take a slant such as this on things without coming rather inconveniently face to face with the majority of people who share no such concern, who fancy the Arts as a National Heritage and as vehicles of Prestige. Life itself means very much the opposite to them, to choose but one example. When in the past I have spoken in small gatherings of what I personally mean by life, the reaction was often one of bemused wonderment. How can this be, I asked myself. What I find most precious, most worthy of effort, discipline and practice, simply does not exist and remains meaningless for most of those around me. But my final judgment on the matter is: all the more reason to be the example of what I value, to personify what I prize.

* * * * * * * *

www.ingramcontent.com/pod-product-compliance
Lightning Source LLC
Chambersburg PA
CBHW060419290526
45791CB00002B/816